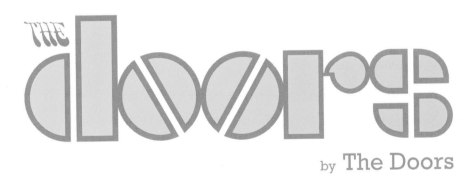

by The Doors

THE doors

by **The Doors** with **Ben Fong-Torres**

forewords by

Henry Rollins
Perry Farrell
Chester Bennington

HYPERION

Library of Congress Cataloging-in-Publication Data

Doors.
  The Doors / by The Doors; with Ben Fong-Torres ; forewords by Henry Rollins, Perry Farrell, Chester Bennington.—1st. ed.
      p. cm.
  Includes bibliographical references.
  ISBN 1-4013-0303-X
  1. Doors (Musical group). 2. Rock Musicians—United States—Biography. I. Title. II. Fong-Torres, Ben.
  ML421.D66 D66 2006
  78242166092 B 22   2006050676

Hyperion books are available for special promotions and premiums. For details contact Michael Rentas, Assistant Director, Inventory Operations, Hyperion, 77 West 66th Street, 12th floor, New York, New York 10023, or call 212-456-0133.

Book design by Melanie Paykos Design

FIRST EDITION

10 9 8 7 6 5 4 3 2 1

DEDICATION AND ACKNOWLEDGMENTS

As the manager of The Doors, as well as one of their biggest fans, I am in the enviable position of being able to help steward and guide the ever-growing legacy of The Doors—Jim Morrison, Robby Krieger, Ray Manzarek, and John Densmore—to old and new generations of Doors fans across the world. How did I end up here?

Two words: Danny Sugerman.

Danny worked for The Doors from the age of fourteen until his passing in January 2005, at the age of fifty. In the end, he was The Doors' co-manager, their biggest fan, the world's most knowledgeable Doors expert, and my business partner. With the exception of Danny's loving wife, Fawn, there was no one more meaningful, important, or with more impact on Danny's life, his outlook, or his vision than Jim Morrison and The Doors. Danny passed from this life as he began in his teens—intimately involved with the musical mentors and heroes he worshiped and protecting, enhancing, and trumpeting their importance, their art, poetry, meaning, and music to a worldwide legion of fanatical followers. Their numbers continue to swell each year, defying the passage of time, culture, and the currency of new artists, leaving many of these artists in their wake. How and why is this?

Hopefully, the book you are about to read will answer some of these questions, and you will get a true insider's look at The Doors. But any history of The Doors would be incomplete without the acknowledgment of Danny Sugerman's unique role in helping to create, protect, and further what I refer to as "The Doors Mystique." I proudly join John Densmore, Robby Krieger, and Ray Manzarek in gratefully dedicating this book to Danny Sugerman. Thank you for a lifetime of devoted service to The Doors and their fans all over the world. We will all miss you.

This book presents the complete story of The Doors, as told by The Doors themselves, with the help of esteemed journalist Ben Fong-Torres. Ben not only interviewed all the surviving Doors as well as Jim Morrison's and Pamela Courson's families, but he also went back over time and compiled all known Morrison interviews that were conducted during Jim's lifetime, inserting Jim's comments, statements, and answers to questions into the narrative as told by the other Doors and a few of their intimates. Throughout the book are photographs of The Doors, many of which have never before been seen outside of The Doors' inner circle.

A book like this is a massive undertaking, and we have been hard at work producing this volume for almost two years. *THE DOORS by The Doors* would have been an impossible task without the dedication, tireless efforts, and long hours dedicated to the project by many, many people. The Doors and I would like to thank the following people for all of their hard work and dedication to this book over these last twenty-four months:

To Bob Miller, Zareen Jaffery, Navorn Johnson, Rachelle Nashner, and all the folks at Hyperion Books for believing, and for their phenomenal respect, intelligence, and thoughtful planning.

To Ben Fong-Torres, for working long hours, interviewing and typing away like a madman, and delivering an incredible book, on impossibly tight deadlines. You have made these pages sing with the essence of what The Doors are really all about.

To Melanie Paykos, Jeff Consoletti, and all over at Melanie Paykos Design for the incredible layout, graphics, and overall design of the book.

To Alan Nevins, Jeff Rabhan, and Jeff Kwatinetz at The Firm and to David Byrnes, Esq. and John Branca, Esq., for helping to carefully guide the shape, vision, and reality of this project from beginning to end.

To Cory Lashever, Todd Gray, and Guy Jordan at The Doors Music Co. for an amazing and tireless job of photo selection, editing, restoration, and layout.

To Steve Baltin, music journalist and author of the final chapter, "The Doors' Musical Impact: Endless," for his dedicated work, interviewing so many of today's current artists.

To Jim Ladd, "The Last DJ", our longtime friend and associate, for countless dedicated hours conducting interview, compiling history and just being there as a sounding board, advisor, fan and trusted voice to all three surviving Doors;

To Steve Young, for use of his beautiful, extensive Doors poster and handbill collection.

To Perry Farrell, Henry Rollins, and Chester Bennington for their wonderful, evocative forewords to this book.

To Admiral George C. Morrison, Anne Morrison, Andy Morrison, Penny Courson, Jerry Mandel, Esq., and Lou Reisman, Esq. for their help, cooperation, encouragement, loving guidance, and amazing recollections that added so greatly to this story.

To Jim Morrison, Ray Manzarek, Robby Krieger, and John Densmore for a lifetime of magic, music, and poetry, and for helping to open the doors of perception for an entire planet.

And, finally, to Doors fans all over the world and across time, who have helped keep the words, music, and message of these phenomenal artists alive, vibrant, and meaningful to each successive generation of new fans. The music, and this book, are for you.

Jeff Jampol
Manager, The Doors
Los Angeles, CA

Waiting for the Sun
Released on Vinyl
July 1968
Elektra/Asylum Records

The Soft Parade
Released on Vinyl
July 1969
Elektra/Asylum Records

Morrison Hotel
Released on Vinyl
February 1970
Elektra/Asylum Records

L.A. Woman
Released on Vinyl
April 1971
Elektra/Asylum Records

FOREWORD BY HENRY ROLLINS

For me, The Doors will always be the first band that made me understand music could do more than provide pleasant distraction. I was very young when I first heard them. The Beatles were great, and I liked The Rolling Stones, but they didn't make me think. I just listened. Then my mother brought home the first Doors album, and just the name of the band got my attention. I was far too young to understand the idea of "doors of perception," I just thought it was a really cool name.

Then I heard the song "Break On Through." It was a revelation. It was so energized and such a break from happy pop music. It was intense, revolutionary music. Even at a young age, I got it, or at least a version of it. I remember spiriting the album away to my room and playing it over and over. It scared me. I would listen to "The End" like I would watch television. I had the feeling that I probably shouldn't be allowed to have this record.

My more powerful connection to The Doors came when I was a teenager and constantly pondering sex, death, and my own life as young people are prone to do. The Doors' albums, especially *Strange Days* really made me feel heavy and thoughtful. In the song "People Are Strange," when Morrison sang, "People are wicked when you're unwanted," helped me understand the feelings of alienation I felt at school. Like many young people, I did not fit in and had no backup, no corner man. The Doors became that for me.

Many people became Doors fans long after the band was gone. The band connected with a whole generation who were not even around when the band was playing. I always thought that was really cool. I felt a closeness to the band and Morrison's voice, having heard the records for so many years. I remember my babysitters talking about Morrison. They would bring Doors records over when they would watch me, and we would listen to them.

To this day, whenever I think of that footage of Morrison walking to the stage—at the Hollywood Bowl, I think it is—and the place erupts as the band goes into "Five to One," it is one of the only times it occurs to me that a song or a band could start a citywide riot. I always wonder what Morrison was thinking at that moment when he was looking at all those people looking back at him with all that excitement and expectation.

Over The Doors' catalog, there are many moments of epiphany, sadness, and beauty that still get me caught up. A song like "Indian Summer" from *Morrison Hotel* is so starkly beautiful and tinged in sorrow and

mortality. It was the lyrics of someone who knew enough to know it was going to end badly, that there was not going to be a way out of the jungle. In the song "The Spy," Morrison sings, "I know your deepest secret fear," perhaps because he knew his own so well. On the cover of the album, Henry Diltz's portrait of the band in the window of the Morrison Hotel, Morrison's expression seems distracted and somewhat hollow. Like a man who was peering into the abyss. The album is so incredibly heavy, one can't imagine the band or the man lasting too much longer. Something had to give—and it did.

For me, The Doors' music relegates so much other music to mere entertainment. Morrison was a dangerous mind. He read books. Huxley, Rimbaud, Artaud, and perhaps Milton. He was an intellectual and artistic anarchist. The dynamics in Morrison's voice, its immersion in the music, the telepathy of the unit, to this day continues to amaze me. I can't think of any other band that would have enabled Morrison to reveal and realize all he did. When talking of The Doors, the sheer presence of Morrison makes us sometimes forget how brilliant Krieger, Densmore, and Manzarek were as players and songsmiths. Morrison needed a highly sympathetic sonic wilderness to wander in, and they were right there for him. It was a perfect fit.

When I see that classic footage of The Doors performing "Light My Fire" on *The Ed Sullivan Show* I try to imagine the unrest it caused all over America that night. To borrow a phrase, the men might not have known, but all the women understood.

Morrison's passing stamped The Doors with a seal of legend and immortality. There was no opportunity for the band to go into the seventies intact. Perhaps that's a good thing. I can't imagine The Doors in the era of disco.

Their music still sounds exciting to me when I listen to it all these years later. It was a different time. Almost primitive compared to the contemporary music world. The Doors played for far bigger stakes than the artists who crowd the airwaves now. They will continue to endure, illuminate, and inspire.

HENRY ROLLINS is a modern-day renaissance man, touring the world and performing with his own Rollins Band as an engaging public speaker and on behalf of the USO. Originally known as the vocalist for the legendary band Black Flag, the Grammy-winning performer, author, and actor currently occupies his time chatting up heavy hitters as the host of IFC's *The Henry Rollins Show*, introducing listeners to hidden gems on his weekly Indie 103.1 radio show, and running his publishing company, *2-13-61*.

FOREWORD BY PERRY FARRELL

A TORCH OF CURIOSITY

Music can transform a boy into a chief. The musician is a witch doctor, willing to step through the bolted conscience to a place of madness, and return again enlightened. As a young boy, when I listened to music, I had a sense of who had truly broken through and who had never left. With the torch of curiosity, I followed these Eagle Chiefs of the outer-world, working with juju, summoning courage.

INDIANS ON A HILLTOP

They say that you can bring three Indians up to the top of a hill, have them sleep up there for a night, and when they return to the village, they will have three different experiences and tell three different tales.

One will say that he was freezing. He was on edge all night—listening to wild animal sounds coming from behind the bushes. He wished he could go back down. By morning he was worn out, swearing he would never go up there again.

Another says that he was tired from the climb. By the time he got up to the top, he simply curled up in his blanket and passed out. He woke with the sun rising, but couldn't remember anything from the night before.

The last one will say that he was enthralled as he looked out over the edge, seeing the most beautiful view of the village below. He saw his people moving about unaware that he was tracking them. He was overcome with love and respect for their lives and the struggles they endured. He felt in harmony. To him, being on the hilltop was awesome. He built a fire and danced around the flame, trying to contact the dead. A lizard came up from a hole in the ground. "What beautiful skin," he thought. "Lucky to meet you. I will take another trip up here and visit you again."

REINVENTING THE WORLD ON THE SPOT

As a boy, the music—and the musicians—formed my identity. Lighting my passion, they guided me through life's great adventure. They were romantic, rebellious, and destructive. They were able to reinvent the world on the spot. I would watch The Doors, and they would cast out wondrous sounds—like wild animals provoking me from behind the bushes. Jim would dance as if circling a fire he had just lit. It made me want to jump up with him and yip and holler, take off my coat and feel the cold breeze shock my bare chest.

HIS VOICE WAS AN ORDER

If it weren't for the music, we would have so little hope, so much less faith. How often we feel like mice, scurrying within a maze constructed by government and corporation, bumping our heads confused into corners, turning in fear.

Who will dare to transform us?
Turn us into lizards to slink away from this sham?
Frighten off the trespassers?
Be present at the night of passage?

A Lizard King, who can do anything... He would return from madness and death with beads around his neck. He could light a fire with the flint in his eyes. His voice was an order. "WAKE UP!" he would say, and the emotionally dead would rise.

RADIO'S DARK NIGHT

What will become of us, now that you are away? Now that the music's over? I have grown up to be a man. I inherited the spirit of the sun from you. How grateful I am that you existed and at one time assumed control over radio's dark night. Will you return in a vast visitation of energy—just as we're about to dream? Pray, tell us, Jim, what goes on at the top?

PERRY FARRELL is one of the most influential and original musical figures in modern rock. Dubbed the "Godfather of Alternative Rock," Farrell put together what would become one of the most influential rock bands of all time, Jane's Addiction, in the early '80s. Jane's Addiction, under the leadership of Farrell, emerged from the L.A. underground music scene, spearheading alternative rock's eventual mainstream attention, acceptance, and success in the 1990s. Creating a new genre and musical movement, Farrell and Jane's Addiction changed modern rock and paved the way for bands such as Nirvana, Pearl Jam, Alice in Chains, and Stone Temple Pilots to follow. Two of Jane's Addiction's platinum-certified albums, 1988's *Nothing's Shocking* and 1990's *Ritual De Lo Habitual,* are considered classics, proving to be important and incredibly influential in the '90s alt-rock scene.

Farrell is also the creator and director of the visionary music festival Lollapalooza launched in 1991. Known for its musical diversity, Lollapalooza was the first to bring together alternative rock, hip-hop, and Electronica. Lollapalooza was instrumental in exposing alternative music formats to the masses and establishing a sense of commonality across an otherwise hopelessly fragmented demographic. Lollapalooza also brought attention to art and provided a platform for numerous environmental and human-rights causes.

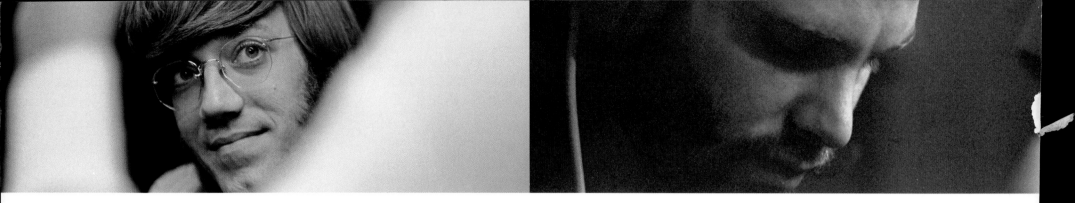

FOREWORD BY CHESTER BENNINGTON

I was thirteen years old when I first heard "Break On Through;" I had no idea who The Doors were or how much their music would have an impact on me. I was an awkward, nerdy, four-eyed funny guy in theater class beginning my completely unsuccessful high school career. Most of my energy was poured into acting and hanging out with the rest of the theater geeks. Music was just starting to become the single most important part of my life.

Although I was a rather unique lad, some of the cool kids still had big enough balls to be seen with me. One of these kids was my friend Jason. He and I started hanging out through a mutual friend at parties, and sometimes he would start jamming on the guitar and singing songs. I was taken aback by how talented he was, and how rare that was, coming from our neighborhood. One day we were hanging out at his house, in his garage, watching Jason play guitar and he starts playing "People Are Strange" and says, "Man, I wish I knew someone who could sing." And I replied, "I can sing. I mean, I think I'm pretty good." He said, "Well that would be awesome—if we only had a mike!" So we proceeded to devise a master plan of juvenile criminal genius. We would first case the church behind his house to see if the preacher or any of his herd were lingering about. When the coast was clear, we used our school IDs to jimmy the lock to the back door of the auditorium. Once inside we immediately noticed a large grand piano next to a four-channel mixer and a microphone connected to a 50-foot-long cable that was wrapped around the piano. That's where our great plan became a major pain in my ass. I must have weaved in and out between the legs of that damn piano a hundred times before I was done. When I had finally retrieved the mike and cable, we ran back to his house and played every Doors song he knew.

We began having our little jam sessions about three times a week, and I was quickly becoming a rabid Doors fan. Jason and I were obsessed with their music, mystery, magic, and mayhem. We would talk about how cool it would be to have the chance to live our lives with reckless abandon and push the envelope to the point of breaking down walls... becoming larger than life.

We started devouring acid, coke, speed, mushrooms, pot, and alcohol, but most of all *acid*. We were actually stupid enough to believe that this made us more like them. We couldn't have been more wrong. We also started becoming quite the party favorite pastime. Performing everything from "Crystal Ship" to "L.A. Woman." In our minds, we might as well have been The Doors themselves. More like Tenacious D does The Doors, only we weren't funny or very good. We were usually so fucked up that everything sounded amazing. These performances started to get people talking about me in the local music scene. Scotty's older brother—the kid Jason and I would jam with every once in a while—asked me if I would come down and practice with a new band he was starting with some kids from the east side. I was blown away that he asked me to go with him, and kind of felt like I might make a fool out of myself, considering I only knew The Doors and a handful of other songs from Nirvana, Jane's Addiction, Black Sabbath, and a few others.

My entire life changed that day. I got the gig as the front man for the band, and as for my friend's brother, he just stopped coming around. Our band's name was SD and His Friends. We sold T-shirts that said: (I'M SEAN DOWDELL'S FRIEND). Quite possibly the stupidest thing ever. We did, however, become popular within the scene of other young bands that all thought their shit didn't stink. We later changed the name by popular demand to Grey Daze, and recorded two CDs that got enough of the right people to hear about me and hooked me up with a little band in Los Angeles called Xero. After about two months, we changed our name to Hybrid Theory, eventually got signed, and changed our name again, to Linkin Park. We've gone on to sell more than thirty six million records in five years and I can't help but feel like The Doors have played a role in all of this. It's amazing how one song at just the right moment can change a person's life.

I remember the first time I played the Whisky a Go Go and thinking to myself, *This is where Jim Morrison stood and performed, music intoxicating everyone in the room.* I thought that life couldn't get any better. If I had died that day, it would have been just fine. Night after night, bands from all over the world come to play the Whisky in the hopes of capturing some of the mojo that's still rising in that room. I wonder, if Jim were still alive today, what he would think of the contribution he and his bandmates have made to the world of rock 'n' roll as we know it. I wonder what he would say to my generation's lack of soul and these cookie cutter labels calling the same thing by a different name. No use in wasting too much energy on shit we'll never know.

I suppose it wouldn't really matter anyway.

When I was asked if I would be interested in participating in this book, I was flattered and excited to be able to talk about a band that means so much to me. The Doors will always stand the test of time. Their story is truly a rock 'n' roll legacy, with beauty, ugliness, passion, and tragedy. When the Doors hit the airwaves, an entire musical movement was destroyed and another was born. One with raw attitude, power, and poetry. They are the most underrated musical powerhouse in rock history. And unlike some that fade away into the abyss, The Doors will always relate to the youth of any era. Music today lacks the power to change people, and more and more kids are raiding their dads' music collections to find anything decent to listen to. I'd be willing to bet that twenty years from now, The Doors will be bigger than they ever were before.

CHESTER BENNINGTON is the vocal firepower behind multiple Grammy–winning group Linkin Park, which has sold more than 36 million records worldwide in just five years. Their first album, *Hybrid Theory*, has been certified platinum eighteen times, and their second album, *Meteora*, ten times. In collaboration with hip-hop artist Jay-Z, they also released the groundbreaking EP *Collision Course*, which garnered rave reviews and features the Grammy Award–winning track "Numb/Encore." In 2005, Linkin Park established Music for Relief with the Red Cross to help aid victims of world catastrophes, the first being the tsunami in Southeast Asia.

INTRODUCTION BY BEN FONG-TORRES

"We're kind of at a crossroads in our career," Jim Morrison told me when I met him in early 1971. "So we'll know, within the next five or six months, what the future will be."

Five months later, in July, he died in Paris.

I flew from San Francisco, which was then home to *Rolling Stone* magazine, where I was a writer and editor, to Los Angeles, to write the obituary.

I don't recall much about those few days I had, holed up in a room that a publicist friend made available. I remember that Salli Stevenson, who wrote for *Circus* magazine and had interviewed Morrison, came by and volunteered herself as an assistant, helping make calls to set up interviews and collecting research materials. I ventured out once or twice to talk with Morrison's friends, and spoke on the phone with many principal players in his life and career, including Jac Holzman, the president of Elektra Records; Elmer Valentine, an owner of the Whisky a Go Go; Bill Siddons, the band's manager who went to Paris and attended the burial. I very vaguely recall writing the article all day and night and into whatever time I had before I had to catch a plane back to San Francisco—with the 6,000-word manuscript in hand. There were no faxes, no computers, no e-mails back then.

And I remember getting one last thing done before I went home to collapse. I wrote the front-page headline, as stark and simple as could be, but with a one-word adjective, tipping my cap to a guy whose work I had enjoyed; whose theatricality I had admired; whose portrayal in the media, late in his career, as a drunken, self-destructive clown I regretted.

JAMES DOUGLAS MORRISON, POET: DEAD AT 27

Having been produced so soon after his death, my obituary offered the same murky information that other reports did. The cause of death was a heart attack, or heart failure. Yes, but … what was the cause of the heart failure itself? Bill Siddons, the band's young manager, spoke about a blood clot, itself the result of "physical abuse." Morrison, he said, "was very strong, but he pushed himself to the limits." Through the years, the mystery of the actual cause of his death has remained just that—a mystery.

Over those years, Morrison and The Doors began to slip from the public's mind, and then, suddenly, they were revived. It was as if Morrison, ever the prankster, was choreographing it himself. First, there was a book of some authority. Only it concluded by leaving one door tantalizingly ajar: Morrison, the authors hinted heavily, might not be dead. Second, there was the use of "The End," the band's ode to love-turned-Oedipal epic, in Francis Ford Coppola's *Apocalypse Now.* Coppola, it turns out, was a classmate of Morrison's—and keyboard player Ray

Manzarek's—in the film department at UCLA in the mid-sixties. Third, there was the matter of what was going on in pop music in the late seventies. It was the era of disco and corporate rock, and, in angry response, punk rock. Fans who adhered to the belief that rock was the music of rebellion gained a new appreciation for those who might be considered the pioneers of punk. The confrontational, theatrical, and even stage-diving Jim Morrison and The Doors absolutely qualified.

And then there was the cover of *Rolling Stone* in September 1981. The magazine had reports on the band's return to prominence; its appeal to a new generation of fans, and its amazing record sales—Elektra Records, an executive there said, "sold more Doors records this year than in any year since they were first released"—and an appreciation of the music by one of its first fans, Paul Williams, founder and editor of the first serious rock magazine, *Crawdaddy!*

And there was an article by Jerry Hopkins, the co-author (with Danny Sugerman) of the book *No One Here Gets Out Alive,* the Morrison biography that helped spark The Doors revival, the book that postulated that the lead singer might very well still be among the living.

His new article was about…well, about the fact that Morrison might still be among the living.

As I said, Morrison might have been behind the scenes, pulling the strings on this latest piece of theater.

And topping off this package of reporting, reviewing, and reliving, there was the cover. The photograph was shot by Gloria Stavers, the late editor of *16* magazine in her New York studio in 1968, of an impossibly handsome Morrison, dark hair, black sweater, dark eyes, black mood, staring intently at the camera, past the headline:

Jim Morrison
He's Hot,
He's Sexy
And He's Dead

The title caused outrage (just what *Rolling Stone* wanted). But, just as it was with the much tamer headline I'd written a decade before, it was true.

Now, since that revival, there've been others. And there've been many more books, recordings, and audio and video compilations, documentaries, and tributes to Morrison and The Doors, many of them by the surviving Doors.

(right) Jim at the Hollywood Bowl, 1968

In one case, Manzarek—Morrison's primary torch-bearer—directed a DVD tribute as a direct response to Oliver Stone's depiction of Morrison in the 1991 film *The Doors.* Among the dozens of books issued over the years, there are many by friends of Morrison's—from Manzarek and Densmore to drinking buddies, lovers, and groupies.

Why, then, another book?

THE DOORS by The Doors is the first presentation of the band's story—not just Jim Morrison's—from the band members themselves. It's time to cede the stage to Ray, the keyboard wizard; Robby, the guitarist who also wrote some of The Doors' greatest hits ("Light My Fire," anybody?); and John, one of the most fluid and expressive drummers of the rock era. Jim is represented by quotes from the many interviews he granted during his five years in the public spotlight. And, for the first time, we have comments from most of his family, including his father, Admiral George ("Steve") Morrison; his sister, Anne Morrison; and his brother, Andy Morrison.

The admiral sat for an interview at his home in San Diego, despite the fact that his beloved wife, Clara, had recently suffered a stroke. (She died several weeks later, in December 2005.) Admiral Morrison and his family have our warmest wishes, along with our gratitude.

I also had the pleasure of meeting Penny Courson, mother of Pamela. Over lunch at El Encanto, a resort hotel in Santa Barbara where she and Pam's father, Columbus "Corky" Courson, live, she added insights and anecdotes to the love story of Pamela and Jim.

Beyond The Doors and family, I've chosen to include a select few intimates—people who worked with the band on the road and in the recording studios and close friends of Jim's, offering fresh revelations about his life—and death—after all these years.

I'm here as your master of ceremonies, and it won't be easy. In many cases, this will be a rock 'n' roll *Rashomon,* through a blurry, hazy, sixties filter.

Although The Doors all agreed to cooperate in this book and to offer new, never-before-published photographs as well as their memories and thoughts about their times together, there are many instances in which they simply cannot agree on when, where, why, and what it all meant.

But hey, it was the sixties, and, unless you were keeping a diary, you are excused.

I will do my best to sort out the facts, such as they are, and to help The Doors to lay out their story in as orderly a fashion as possible. But, truth be told (or not), no promises can be made. Mysteries will abound, and remain. About the only thing to be certain of is that, forty years after they came together in Venice and Santa Monica, they and their music remain a mesmerizing part of rock 'n' roll past and present. Ever present.

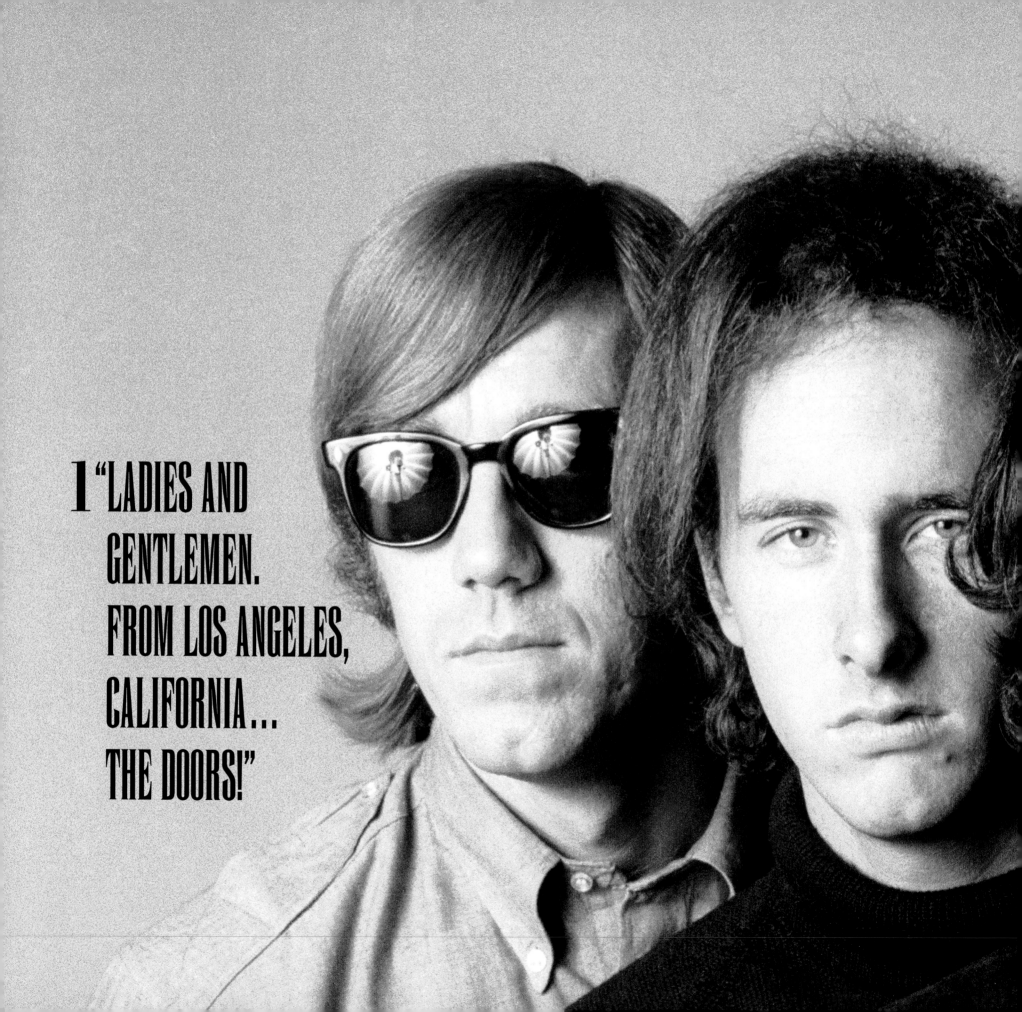

1 "LADIES AND GENTLEMEN. FROM LOS ANGELES, CALIFORNIA... THE DOORS!"

1 "LADIES AND GENTLEMEN. FROM LOS ANGELES, CALIFORNIA...THE DOORS!"

RAY MANZAREK

That's how it always was. "The Doors." Never "Jim Morrison and The Doors." Well, once, but Morrison himself quickly got the stage announcer to make the necessary correction.

The Doors were a band of equals. The spotlight shone more brightly on one of them, but the music required all four; those four.

We begin with Ray Manzarek, the oldest member, the one who recognized in Jim Morrison a poet with the makings of a lead singer for a rock band.

Manzarek lives in Napa, in California wine country, with Dorothy, his wife since 1967. Their son, Pablo, is grown and gone.

Ray: I was born in Chicago, the South Side, on February 12, 1939. My father, Raymond Daniel Manzarek Sr., was a tool-and-dye man, a machinist, at International Harvester in Chicago, and was a good union man. My mother was Helen Kolenda, and there were three boys. I was the oldest, and then my brother Rick, and my youngest brother was Jim. So there were the three boys and my father, and my mother was absolutely wonderful taking care of her four men.

My parents were both second-generation Polish kids from the South Side of Chicago; they grew up in an area called Bridgeport, and in Bridgeport was the legendary Maxwell Street. My father would take me down—I must have been about six or seven—to Maxwell Street on a Sunday, and Maxwell Street was the world's largest swap meet/outdoor market, just more stuff than you could ever imagine. The exciting thing for me was the music that was being played by itinerant street musicians with their little hats, out to make a couple of bucks if they could, and it was a revelation to my seven-year-old brain. It was the first time I ever heard music with such passion, such energy. Only later did I realize what that music was: the blues.

Then, as a young teen, I heard the blues on the radio, and I heard Muddy Waters, Howling Wolf, Magic Sam, John Lee Hooker, and Jimmy Reed. I tell you, that South Side of Chicago radio saved my soul.

My parents were into music because, being down there in that black-white area, it was one of those melting-pot things. So my parents were definitely into all of that blues stuff. My father played a little bit of acoustic guitar and a great ukulele. And my mother loved to sing. Then, when the kids got old enough, the kids would sing too.

When I was seven or eight, they bought a huge German upright piano and said, "Raymond, you're gonna take piano lessons." So I went for my first piano lesson and it was down Archer Avenue and it was right next to Strauss's Bakery. I cannot remember what the man's name was, but he *vas a little German man,* or a middle European of some sort or another.

(previous spread) From The Doors' first studio photo shoot with photographer Joel Brodsky, Lower East Side, New York, 1966

(below) The Doors ready to "Break On Through," New York, 1967

(**left**) Ray stationed in Korat, Thailand, 1963

My father takes me there; it is Saturday morning. We go upstairs into this semi-darkened room, and he has an upright piano, sits me down in front of it, and it's dark, and I don't like this, and he turns on a little light above where the music would rest. And there are these lines, five lines and below it another five lines, two strange, arcane symbols on the left hand side, treble clef and bass clef, and then there are these dots on these lines, bars going up and down, vertical lines, horizontal bars, and little dots in these little spaces. I think, "What is this? I need a Captain Midnight decoder ring for this; this is ridiculous." And he says, "Raymont, Raymont, zis is moo-sic." He says, "Look here, zis is mittle C, see zis note here." And it's a note with a line through it, and it's below the clef or below those five lines, and then he plunks the piano, "Zis is mittle C." And he holds my hand and I play the middle C. Then he says, "Now vee vill play: C D E, E D C, D E C." So he showed me the notes, and the song went, stepping up, stepping down, then a skip, and I thought, "Yes, I see it. I can do this."

And he gave me this songbook, and I developed some sort of proficiency. My mother and father said I had to practice two times a day, a half hour after school and a half hour after dinner, and do homework. So I'm finally getting the hang of it, and one song that really got me was "Good King Wenceslas"—it's like the Modern Jazz Quartet, and it was that dark modal thing that I was digging. I didn't know modal, I didn't know anything; all I knew was, "Oh, that's cool." My mother heard that, and she's right there singing. So I'm accompanying my mother. And it was like, "God, this is kind of cool. I kinda dig this."

After I took lessons with the little German, my mother and father realized that I had to get something a little bit more advanced. They took me to Bruno Michelotti, a young, hip bandleader and piano player who had cool jazz, swing, and dance band arrangements, and he gave piano lessons, and he was the guy who taught me how to play jivey, jazzy stride piano, and how to read chord changes. He was a great teacher.

I went to an all-boys high school, St. Rita High. High school was never a trauma for me. I wasn't in with the popular crowd—there *was* no popular crowd—and I wasn't one of the nerds. At St. Rita, it was like two thousand guys, nobody cares.

But I never got laid until I went to DePaul University in Chicago. My first girlfriend, Pat Milligan, was a great chick, a beatniky girl. Beatniks were happening at the time, and we had a sexual awakening experience and just had sex as often as we possibly could.

Beatniks represented freedom. Kids turn seventeen or so and are looking for that sense of commitment and a sense of freedom and a sense of living for something beyond yourself, and that's what the beatniks were for me. They were guys and women, great female writers, Lenore Kandel (*The Love Book*) and Diane di Prima (editor of the literary newsletter, the *Floating Bear*). Michael McClure, Jack Kerouac, Allen Ginsberg, who wrote "Howl," and John Clellon Holmes, who wrote a book called *Go*, which was the beatniks' mantra—*go man go, go.* And everything I read about the beatniks and by the beatniks was street, real, holy, spiritual, and full of adventure and excitement, a whole new way of being a nonconformist, a non-fifties way of being, and I couldn't wait to get out to the West Coast to experience some of that beatnik action.

I graduated from DePaul University and got my bachelor's degree in June 1960, and by September, I was enrolled in the UCLA Law School.

California represented a magical land where there was warmth, palm trees, girls in bikinis, West Coast jazz, and eternal sunshine.

I was going to be an attorney. I was going to defend the common man, and as we would say today, I was going to be a *liberal* attorney. I was going to be Clarence Darrow in *Inherit the Wind*.

I was at UCLA a couple of weeks and said, "This is ridiculous. Who cares?" It was so involved and so silly, with all the cases that you have to read, case after case after case after case, and then do a brief. No way. So I decided that it would be film school for me. A combination of all the arts: photography, acting, writing, and music. The art form of the twentieth century.

Then, I had a broken love affair at UCLA. I was totally distraught, and I said, "Hey, you know what I can do? I can get my military service out of the way." This was 1962, before Vietnam—the cusp of Vietnam. And then, I thought, I'd come back and get into film school.

1 "LADIES AND GENTLEMEN. FROM LOS ANGELES, CALIFORNIA...THE DOORS!"

(below) Father & Son: Ray on piano, Ray Sr. on guitar, Chicago, 1950

And the U.S. Army sent me to Thailand. And in Thailand, there's something called a "Thai stick." I wind up smoking Thai weed with a guy who turns out to be an MP in the Thai army, in the lushness of the jungle in central Thailand.

After serving a year and a half, Manzarek and the Army both realized it was a relationship that never should have been entered into in the first place. Ray's captain in Okinawa said to him, "Manzarek, some people are just not meant for military service. You are a rake and a reprobate. Not to mention sexually perverse. We don't need your type in the U.S. Army." Ray was gone in a flash, returning to UCLA, and to its film school.

Ray: Jim Morrison and I were both in the film department, and we wound up having some classes together. We got together through a circle of friends and started hanging out, getting stoned. Jim and I hit it off right away and talked about music, film, literature, and philosophy while getting stoned together—along with at least half of the students in the film department. That's when marijuana first hit in my life, in the early sixties when people really first started smoking it. The stoners in the film department all went crazy with wild ideas.

We were into the Nouvelle Vague at that time, the French New Wave: Jean-Luc Godard and François Truffaut started happening in France. And Federico Fellini happened in Italy, then Ingmar Bergman in Sweden, Satyajit Ray in India, and, in Japan, Akira Kurosawa and a couple of others. Cinema was becoming a worldwide thing. And Jim and I both had a class with Josef von Sternberg, the director of *The Blue Angel* and the inventor of Marlene Dietrich. He was an amazing man, and I think of him as partly responsible for the darkness and the mystery of The Doors.

All of a sudden everybody was getting high and making experimental movies, and then out of England, what should come along in '64 but The Beatles and the whole rock 'n' roll thing. Incredible. Far out. And then The Rolling Stones. The Stones were the really big influence, in hip America. They were dope smokers and they were playing rock 'n' roll music. At that point Jim and I thought, "Wow, we could play rock 'n' roll music," just like that. That's how The Doors really got started. The Rolling Stones blew our minds.

Jim: In a way, we came along at a weird time because we came kind of at the tail end of the rock revival from England. You know, they'd already done it. So everyone was saying, "Hey, look at that, they did it." I think it was the success of those English groups that gave hope to a lot of musicians over here, saying, *"Pssh,* we can do the same thing!"

Ray: So I'm at UCLA, and I'm living with Dorothy Fujikawa, who I'd met in a class, Beginning Drawing. We're madly in love. We had both smoked marijuana and then heard about LSD, and all of a sudden somebody actually had some LSD.

I took LSD and said, "Oh my God, I'm alive on the planet; I'm a human being, alive on planet earth." For the first time in my life I understood what it meant to be alive. I was lying in the front of Frank Lisciandro's house. Frank and his wife, Kathy, and Dorothy and I. I was outside in the grassy area and I *felt* the globe of the earth. I was lying on my back with my hands and legs completely spread out and I said, "My God, I'm on a globe." And I thought, "This globe is spinning through outer space at a thousand miles an hour, spinning around and around, taking 365 days to go around the sun." Those are the kinds of realizations that we all came to on psychedelics. And then we looked at religion, the predominant religion being Christianity. I looked at my religion and said, "Jesus Christ is talking about love!" That is exactly what the hippies were talking about. Make love, not war. And *that* was the sixties.

And then Jim and I both graduated from UCLA in May of '65. Jim received his B.A. in film and I received my master's. "Now what?" I said to Jim. "I don't know about you," he said, "but I'm going to New York." I was shocked. I thought, "What a bummer. We had had too much fun together."

"New York?" I said. "Why?"

"I don't know. I just feel like going to New York." He had no concrete plans, no job prospects. "I'm just gonna go," he told me. "Maybe get in with Jonas Mekas's 'film culture' kind of people." In other words, the avant garde.

"Where you gonna live?"

(below) Four-year-old Jim, already standing tall

"I don't know."

"How can I get a hold of you?"

He looked up into the sky and spoke slowly. "Come to Greenwich Village and you'll find me."

I thought I'd never see him again.

JIM MORRISON

**I am a Scot, or so
I'm told. Really
The heir of Mystery
    Christians**

Snake in the Glen

**The child of a
    Military family…**

**I rebelled against church
   After phases of
    Fervor
I curried favor in school
   & attack'd the teachers
    I was given a
    Desk in the corner**

    **I was a fool
      &
   The smartest kid
     In class**

In the biography form he filled out for Elektra Records, Jim Morrison told the truth, mostly. He was born, he said, on December 8, 1943, in Melbourne, Florida. He attended St. Petersburg Junior College in St. Petersburg, Florida, Florida State University in Tallahassee, and UCLA. His ambitions included making films, and his favorite actor and actress were Jack Palance and Sarah Miles. Favorite musical

(below) Seven-year-old Jim, dressed as an Indian for Halloween (left), with brother, Andy (right)

artists included Frank Sinatra, Elvis Presley, The Beach Boys, The Kinks, and a fellow act on Elektra, Love. He was single, he said, and his family members were dead.

Hey, I did say mostly true.

Adm. George (Steve) Morrison: I'd never heard that. I had the feeling that he felt we'd just as soon not be associated with his career, and stay in the background. He knew I didn't think rock music was the best goal for him. Maybe he was trying to protect us.

Jim: I don't want to involve anyone unless they want it…When we're born we're all footprinted and so on. I guess I said my parents were dead as some kind of joke. I have a brother, too, but I haven't seen him in about a year. I don't see any of them.

Besides the brother Morrison mentioned (Andy, who was six years younger), Jim had a sister, Anne, three years his junior.

Anne: I thought he was doing that to separate himself from my parents. My dad was in the Navy; he had his own life, and I don't think Jim wanted to involve them at all. He was a real gentleman. He knew he was going to be doing things that would not have been approved by the family. I don't think he wanted the responsibility of his behavior reflecting on anybody else, and he separated himself completely. He liked mystique, too. He didn't want to be from *somewhere.*

Robby Krieger: He wanted there to be an aura of mystery about the band. He didn't want people to know about his background or where he came from. He told people his parents were dead not because he hated them; I think it was more because he wanted people to think he came from outer space or something.

Adm. Morrison: My career was fairly typical of a flight aviator. When I graduated from the Naval Academy, it was February of 1941, and most of us went to ships in the Pacific. Mine was tied up in Pearl Harbor. We had a nice year there; I had a chance to meet my future wife (Clara Clarke), and there were a lot of social activities.

After the attack on Pearl Harbor, I wanted to get into the war, so I applied for flight training and for submarine training; I got my orders to Pensacola first, so I went to flight training there. I went to finish my training in Melbourne, Florida. And that's where Jim was born.

Andy: Dad was a straight shooter from a small town in Leesburg, Florida. My grandmother taught him to play the piano. She was semi-professional; she played the organ in silent movie houses.

Anne: We had other rebels and musicians in the family besides Jim. My mother's father was a Socialist, and they lived in a Socialist camp in Louisiana. And my grandmother on father's side had perfect pitch and played piano. And my aunt played piano.

Andy: All through growing up, the aviators had a lot of parties and a lot of drinking. There was always a big crowd around the piano with my dad playing popular songs that he could pick up by ear.

I remember some of the parties got pretty loose—but not my dad. My dad was always a Southern gentleman. After about two or three gin and tonics, he'd start drinking straight tonic water.

Anne: My father was quite a showman himself. My parents had so much fun. They had wonderful parties, put on acts. We'd watch them from upstairs. Singing...playing honky-tonk stuff, the hits of the day.

Andy: And you know when we were in Claremont, Jim was class president at Long Fellow. If I was kindergarten, he was fifth or sixth grade, I think it might have been sixth grade because he was the boy scout, he'd go out with my dad to Miramar and get his merit badges, so he was into that kind of stuff.

But more than anything, Jim was into reading, writing, and drawing.

Jim: I think around the fifth or sixth grade I wrote a poem called "The Pony Express." That was the first I can remember. It was one of those ballad-type poems. I never could get it together, though. I always wanted to write, but I figured it'd be no good unless somehow the hand just took the pen and started moving without me really having anything

to do with it. Like, automatic writing. But it just never happened. I wrote a few poems, of course.

Indians scattered on dawn's highway bleeding.

Ghosts crowd the young child's fragile eggshell mind.

The first time I discovered death...me and my mother and father, and my grandmother and grandfather were driving through the desert at dawn. A truckload of Indian workers had either hit another car or something—there were Indians scattered all over the highway, bleeding to death. I was just a kid, so I had to stay in the car while my father and grandfather went to check it out. I didn't see nothing—all I saw was funny red paint and people lying around, but I knew something was happening because I could dig the vibrations of the people around me, and all of a sudden I realized that they didn't know what was happening any more than I did. That was the first time I tasted fear...and I do think, at that moment, the souls of those dead Indians—maybe one or two of 'em—were just running around, freaking out, and just landed in my soul, and I was like a sponge, ready to sit there and absorb it.

Adm. Morrison: He was older than four. It was a bright sunny day in New Mexico. We were driving in Albuquerque, toward Taos. We went by several Indians. One of them was crying. It did make an impression on him. He always thought about that crying Indian.

Anne: We lived in Albuquerque, and we would go out to reservations or the mountains on occasion. The Navy did things for the Navajos, and we'd go out there for the day. We lived there when I was two, and he was six. And then again when I was eight, so he was eleven or twelve.

He enjoyed telling that story, and exaggerating it. He says we saw a dead Indian on the side of the road, and I don't even know if that's true. He enjoyed having the spirit of the Indian in him as part of his persona. He liked the Shaman concept.

Jim: And it's not a ghost story, man. It's something that really means something to me.

Young Jim was a precocious kid. He liked messing with his siblings, teasing Anne, and doing much more to Andy. He liked to pull pranks in school; he enjoyed reading Mad *magazine and drew cartoons of his own, usually adding a sadistic edge, with an emphasis on bodily functions and sex.*

Andy: Jim just liked to have a lot of fun; he had a good sense of humor. He used to pick up some rocks and give you the count of ten, and you'd better start running. And he would throw some rocks—but not to do a lot of damage. Or, in the swimming pool, he'd grab you and say, "Let's see if you can hold your breath for a minute." And then hold you under water. Well, he might hold you down there for ten or fifteen seconds. One time when I was in junior high, he stopped some kid walking down the street the other way and said, "Hey, my brother wants to fight you." He wanted to see a reaction. He thought it was funny. And he also thought it was funny, when you were on the couch watching TV, to come over and sit on your face and fart. I don't think that's too unusual for an older brother.

Because of his father's career, Jim and the family were constantly on the move; between grammar school and high school, Jim lived in six different cities from California to Virginia.

Anne: I think my brothers and I were pretty close because we moved a lot. Whenever we moved, we were the only ones we knew, so we were good friends for a long time, until we got to know other people.

Adm. Morrison: He was independent-minded; he had his own ideas and thoughts. I had no arguments with that. We didn't have any quarrels. I knew he didn't agree with some of the things I did, but he didn't try and make an issue of it, and I tried to give him the same consideration.

Andy: Until he got to be in high school, he wasn't that rebellious, but my dad's right; he did give him a lot of leeway. My dad was gone about half the time. In those days they had about nine-month cruises, and I think my brother and my mother had a relationship that—Jim was the little man around the house.

But did he do his share of chores?

1 "LADIES AND GENTLEMEN. FROM LOS ANGELES, CALIFORNIA…THE DOORS!"

Andy: Most of the time, up until in high school, like in Alameda (California), he started to get a little more independent. I remember one thing; I don't remember what the argument was, my mother was pissed and they were starting to get into a fight in the living room and I stood back and didn't know what side to take, but Jim was not as serious as my mother. My mother had a hard streak; she could be pretty ornery.

She was slapping at Jim and he started laughing and got out his ballpoint pen and started drawing on her arm and this just infuriated her and he was just laughing. I remember her screaming, "You don't fight fair! You don't fight fair!" And he's taking the ballpoint pen up and down her arm.

Anne: We did not argue. That's the way we were raised. When we were in high school, Jim was becoming more unusual, compared to the rest of people in families. He used to go buy clothes at the Goodwill. That *was* a clash, the clothes he would like to wear. He'd come home with some very strange things. Pointy shoes and things no one else's children would wear.

Penny Courson: His mother mentioned that she would give him money to buy a shirt and he'd go down to Goodwill and buy one for a quarter. And then he'd take the rest of the money and go down to the neighborhood where the jazz bands were and listen to jazz.

Anne: And when he was coming home from college, he would come home with long hair, and that wasn't acceptable in our house.

In Alameda, a city connected to Oakland by a tunnel, Jim Morrison was only a couple of bus rides away from San Francisco, which beckoned from across the Bay Bridge.

It was 1957, and the fourteen-year-old Jim began to split his loyalties between Mad *magazine's sick and satiric humor and the poetry and rebellion of the emerging beatnik scene in San Francisco's North Beach. Jim devoured Jack Kerouac's* On the Road.

After a year, the family moved again—this time to Alexandria, Virginia.

IQ of 149. He was prone to stunts and pranks at school and elsewhere. He now had girlfriends, and teased and taunted them, too.

Anne: In high school, he would just leave school sometimes to go to Washington, D.C., to go to the library. One time he told the teacher he was having a brain tumor removed and walked out of class. The teacher called my mom to ask how he was doing. She didn't know what she was talking about. "Well, the brain tumor…"

"He doesn't have a brain tumor!"

Andy: He got along with the folks and they always gave him these rooms—like in Alexandria, he was in the basement with his own exit, a stairway out the back. In Alameda, he had a whole floor to himself. My dad gave him a lot of room so if he wanted to go out and do stuff, he had easy access.

Anne: He was an avid reader, and he had a notebook in high school. He'd learn a new word and write a whole story around it. He wrote all the time. I just thought he'd be a beatnik and be poor all his life.

Jim: "Horse Latitudes" I wrote when I was in high school. I kept a lot of notebooks through high school and college, and then when I left school, for some dumb reason—maybe it was wise—I threw them all away. There's nothing I'd rather have in my possession now than those two or three lost notebooks. I was thinking of being hypnotized or taking sodium Pentothal to try to remember, because I wrote in those books night after night. But maybe if I'd never thrown them away, I'd never have written anything original, because they were mainly accumulations of things that I'd read or heard, like quotes from books. I think if I'd never gotten rid of them I'd never have been free.

I was a good student; read a lot. But I was always talking when I wasn't supposed to, so they made me sit at a special table—nothing bad enough to get expelled for. I got through school. Went to Florida State University mainly because I couldn't think of anything else to do.

Anne: When he graduated from high school, he asked our parents for the complete works of (Friedrich) Nietzsche. I think my parents thought it was rather strange. Most kids want to go and do something fun, or get

1 "LADIES AND GENTLEMEN, FROM LOS ANGELES, CALIFORNIA…THE DOORS!"

Andy: When Jim graduated, he didn't want to go to the graduation. Also, he didn't do anything for college, so my parents did it for him. From there, I think he saw that he was more than junior college material, and he got himself into Florida State, in Tallahassee, where he got on the dean's list.

Once, I was having trouble with school. I was a poor reader. He would give me lists of books I should read. I was about fifteen, and he had me read *Studs Lonigan* by James Farrell. And it was about a fifteen-year-old kid growing up in Chicago who liked to play football and ran around, so I could relate to it. And it was good literature, so then I realized that, besides *The Red Badge of Courage,* there was some good reading out there. That helped me a lot.

After he got on the dean's list, he decided he had a plan, and he wanted to go to film school at UCLA.

Jim: I finished up at UCLA. The only reason I did it is because I didn't want to go in the Army, and I didn't want to work—and that's the damned truth.

In virtually every biography of Morrison, it's been said that he went to UCLA without his parents' knowledge, approval, or assistance. His family disagrees.

Adm. Morrison: That suited me fine. I was delighted when Jim decided to go to UCLA. I thought his talents lay in that line of work, and that he'd get contacts there.

Anne: I think the decision was all his, to go and study film.

Andy: And my parents paid the tuition. Jim was supposed to write a letter once a month to get his allowance, so he did. He'd write these letters and we'd sit around, the whole family, and read them, and he'd just make up a crock of shit like being at the movies and the place caught on fire and he calmed everybody down by getting up onstage and singing a song. So we knew it was all horseshit and we'd look forward to his next monthly read.

Jim: The good thing about film is that there aren't any experts. There's no authority on film. Any one person can assimilate and contain the whole history of film in himself, which you can't do in other arts. There are no experts, so, theoretically, any student knows almost as much as any professor.

The only film I made (at UCLA) was a film that was questioning the film process itself, so it was a film about film. I had a lot of people watching the film in a room, and then I showed people watching television and then filled the whole screen up with things that were shot off television…A few people liked it, and most people were indifferent to it.

Ray: I remember going over to Jim's apartment and hanging out. And Jim had this big wall of books, and one of Jim's tricks, Jim would say, "Take a book off the shelf, I'll turn my back, you read me a couple of lines, a paragraph, whatever, and I'll tell you what the book is and who the author is." And Jim would bet you a six-pack of some Tecate or Corona, and by god Jim Morrison drank free beer nineteen out of twenty times.

Andy: We got transferred to London in 1965 [Adm. Morrison was on the staff of the commander in chief, Naval Operations, Europe], and my dad and Jim had a falling out because Jim wanted to go into music or borrow some money. And I didn't hear from him for two years.

Adm. Morrison: He called me and told me he was going on the road with a rock band. I told him it was ridiculous. I said, "You're not a singer. You can't sing." He never had. Driving across country, we all liked to sing. It was just to pass the time. I didn't think any of us had a voice. I said, "You're on the wrong track here. Get yourself a job. That's not a job."

In another telling of this incident, Jim is said to have informed his parents of his rock band plans in one of his letters to his family in London. Adm. Morrison reportedly wrote back, expressing disappointment that, after paying his tuition for four years, his son was starting a band. "I think it's a crock," he's said to have written.

The Morrisons, father and son, never saw each other again.

(below) Man Bites Dog: Jim and Thor
(Ray's brother's dog) on an abalone hunt,
1965

JOHN DENSMORE

Drummers are stuck in the back, behind the lead singer and the guitarists, behind the spots. Or they're the butt of jokes, as in Spinal Tap. *But in his essay about The Doors, on the occasion of their induction into the Rock and Roll Hall of Fame, Paul Rothchild, who was their producer for their first five albums, brought their drummer up front—if only for a moment. He wrote, simply:*

John Densmore, a jazz drummer with an unbeatable knack for shamanic rhythm and theatrical timing…the band's tireless engine.

John: My mom is Margaret Peggy—maiden name, Walsh; married name, Densmore. She was a native Californian from a good Catholic family, and she went to Beverly Hills High during the Depression and became a librarian. When she was sixteen, Ray Blaisdale Densmore moved in next door. He had driven his family across the country from York, Maine, to the suburbs of Los Angeles when he was only twelve. At twenty-three, Ray attended USC in pursuit of a degree in architecture and moonlighted as an actor with the Santa Monica Players. Mom was also making money as a commercial artist. She was—is still a painter at ninety-one, but basically a housewife who raised three kids: my older sister, Ann, me, and my younger brother, Jim.

My father, Ray Densmore, worked day and night to get through school, and graduated when the Depression started, but he did all right as an architect.

My parents were so good at picking up a pencil and scribbling something, I was intimidated by that. But I've always loved music, and they encouraged it.

Music hypnotized me and transported me out of my little suburban bedroom into fantasyland. At eight and a half years old I asked my parents for a piano and lessons. They obliged and rented an old upright. I took to the instrument immediately. I liked improvising on songs I had learned, rather than learning new ones.

I went to Daniel Webster Junior High in West Los Angeles, and I said I wanted to be in the band, and I'd play any instrument, I don't care. So

I was going to play clarinet, but I had braces so my teeth were being pushed out by the clarinet. The orthodontist said, "Nope!"

The band director suggested drums. So I said, "OK, drums."

In high school, I graduated to the marching band with those stupid uniforms. I loved the feeling of power I got from playing with forty other musicians, no matter how amateurish.

I worked my way up from bass drummer to cymbal player and, finally, first snare drummer. To develop a solid sense of time, learning the basic drum beats first (called the "grandfather beat" in Native American cultures) is of primary importance. I was earning the right to play the complicated rhythmic nuances of the snare parts. When playing trap drums or the entire drum set, you put it all together and play all the percussion instruments at once: snare, bass, tom-toms, and cymbals. I was fortunate to learn the drum instruments separately, so that I had a thorough understanding when I put them all together.

What really intrigued me was playing timpani in the orchestra, because they provided the very dramatic climaxes of the simplified classical compositions, and I liked that—the fortissimo of it all. You had to count a lot of bars when you were drumming with the orchestra. In other words, just wait.

In my second year of high school I was asked to join a pop band. My mother painted our logo on the front of my bass drum: TERRY AND THE TWILIGHTERS. All the other guys in the band were from Catholic families like me, but they went to parochial schools. After I threw up in the first grade of our local Catholic school, my parents thought public school might offer less pressure. So I ended up attending University High School, or "Uni," as we called it, but I couldn't get out of catechism classes on Saturdays. The Twilighters started playing the Catholic-school circuit around Los Angeles, and I found I could impress the girls with my drumming. I could feel everybody's eyes on me, and I milked the attention with melodramatic self-importance. I thought I was a pretty good drummer and, with an audience, I was inspired to concentrate even more.

1 "LADIES AND GENTLEMEN. FROM LOS ANGELES, CALIFORNIA…THE DOORS!"

(top) John and Jim, playing with the neighbors' dog, West Los Angeles, 1948

(bottom) John and his brother Jim, Los Angeles, 1956

(below) John sporting a pompadour in his sophomore high school yearbook photo

Then I got into jazz and became a snob. I saw all of the jazz musicians, every one. I got a fake ID in Tijuana at age sixteen to play drums in bars, as well as at weddings and bar mitzvahs. And it got me into Shelly's Manne-Hole, the L.A. jazz club, and I saw Miles, Coltrane, Art Blakey, Bill Evans, Les McCann—there's not a jazz musician you could name that I haven't seen, sat right next to, watched play. So that was really my thing.

In high school, my grades had been average in all my classes other than music and sports, and no major universities were seeking a snare-drum player for their marching bands.

So by the fall of 1963, it was off to Santa Monica City College, where I majored in apathy and changing majors. First it was music, but I thought I could never make a living at it. Therefore, I switched to business. After getting a D in accounting—the second time around—I thought someone was trying to tell me something. Maybe college wasn't for me.

But music was in my blood. I didn't have time for studies because I was hanging out at the music building jamming with the cats. The head of the department used to storm across the hallway.

"Could you guys please turn it down?" he would plead. "I'm trying to rehearse the junior orchestra."

Despite all the hassling, we were doing something right. We were the foundation of a mother of a marching band. By the middle of my second semester, our SMCC band had been accepted in the citywide competition at the Rose Bowl. We marched through the streets of Pasadena to the stadium—and to victory! Best band in the city!

But by 1964, the breakaway from family, and from tradition, had begun. I was feeling a pull from suburban L.A. into the clubs of Hollywood. That summer, something amazing started happening to the music scene in L.A. New clubs were opening up down the Sunset Strip: Fred C. Dobbs, the Trip, Bito Lido's, and the Brave New World. The bands that played there weren't into Top-40 music. They played their own stuff, at deafening volume. Every night I could, I would go to Hollywood with a high school friend, Grant Johnson, and hang out at the clubs until two or three in the morning. There was no age limit because they didn't serve alcohol. My parents were sure I was going to end up in the gutter.

By now, The Beatles had come along, and I was curious. I thought they were homosexual, but their melodies were great, and they were so different. I certainly was aware of Elvis and the roots of rock 'n' roll, but with this English New Wave coming through, I thought, "What's this? This is interesting." Maybe I could do something like that, you know.

Grant and I moved out of our parents' homes and into a developing hippie community in Topanga Canyon, which was a beautiful, tree-filled, mountainous area forty minutes from Hollywood. My parents agreed to pay half of the $70-a-month rent as long as I was going to college, so I transferred to San Fernando Valley State College, just over the hill from Topanga.

Inevitably, school took a backseat to going out to jazz clubs and, soon enough, sitting in on jam sessions … and taking our first hits of LSD. Acid had more of a kick than the stale wafer I swallowed on my first holy communion. LSD was a *direct* experience with God that I felt, or at least something otherworldly or mystical.

A few weeks later, I met—or re-met—Robby Krieger. I'd seen him around at Uni High. I remember seeing him driving his parents' fancy Plymouth car and using a credit card to buy gas. I thought he was a rich kid with an attitude. He was also very quiet, but it didn't take long to realize that his shyness was due to sensitivity and gentleness, not snobbery. Ideas were always spinning in his head. While everyone else was listening to Top 40, Robby was digging Paul Butterfield, Robert Johnson, and Jimmy Reed. Plus playing flamenco guitar.

Soon we were taking acid together. [LSD had not yet been made illegal.]

In April of 1965, there was a party and Robby came with a couple of friends—and his stash. I found out that Robby had been busted for grass (I was never popped, despite what was reported in one Doors biography). He was riding in his car, smoking a marijuana cigarette, and got pulled over. I wondered if Robby was a little too wild to become my friend.

At the party, I met Bill Wolff, a friend of Robby's who was a guitar player with a great sense of humor. We hit it off real well, and, by the end of the evening, Robby, Grant, Bill, and I decided to form a band and call it the Psychedelic Rangers.

1 "LADIES AND GENTLEMEN. FROM LOS ANGELES, CALIFORNIA...THE DOORS!"

By the spring of 1965, the Beach Boys were sweeping the charts with their surfer songs, and there were mumblings about our boys fighting in a far-off country called Vietnam. It seemed light-years away from sunny Southern California.

Our first rehearsal was held in the living room of Robby's parents' house. We wrote a song called "Paranoia" in a folk-rock style, with absurd lyrics by Grant like "that black-and-white fever has got you uptight," referring to the cops.

A friend of Grant's had an eight-millimeter home movie camera, so we decided to make a little movie of our potential hit song. The film began with a shot of me jumping off a ledge, landing on my drum stool and starting the first beats of the song. By the time it was over, Grant had tipped his electric piano over, and we had wrecked our equipment and were laughing hysterically (and this was well before we'd seen The Who!).

The band was crumbling from lack of gigs, but we still hung out together. Robby got Bill, Tommy, and me interested in taking a meditation course.

Robby: I was tired of doing acid all the time, and some friends of mine had gone to India and found this Maharishi Mahesh Yogi. This was before he was ever over here, or with The Beatles. He came over and gave a talk at this guy's house, with twelve people, and that was the beginning of the TM [Transcendental Meditation] movement.

John: I liked the "separate reality" perspective that acid had given me, but I knew that this substance was so strong and powerful that it would wrack my nervous system if I took it a lot. My intuition told me to plan my environment (going to the mountains or the beach) before taking a trip, which helped eliminate fear from my experience.

And so Robby and I decided to go to this meditation class. We went to some preliminary meetings and listened to a mellow man in a business suit. His name was Jerry Jarvis, and his eyes seemed to express a remarkable inner contentment.

After completing the series of meetings, we were on our way to being initiated into Maharishi Mahesh Yogi's Transcendental Meditation. We joked while driving over about how we'd stumbled onto instant nirvana for only $35. They asked us to bring flowers, fruit, and a white handkerchief. We would each receive an individual mantra, an Indian Sanskrit word that we were supposed to repeat mentally. Our teachers instructed us not to speak it aloud or write it down; it could lose its power if we did.

I got dizzy during my first meditation, so I was anxious to go to the follow-up meeting the night after our initiation into TM. Everyone was sharing his experiences of calm and serenity while Jarvis explained what goes on when one meditates, to make sure we were doing it correctly.

Still, not too much happened when I meditated. There were no colored lights or explosions. Though I was expecting the same quick, startling effect as my LSD experiences, in the back of my mind I knew that most Eastern religions spoke of years of rigorous meditation before illumination or enlightenment, if then.

At the follow-up meeting, a blond guy with a Japanese girlfriend by his side kept raising his hand and saying, "No bliss, no bliss!" He acted as if he had been ripped off. I think he expected to become Buddha on the first day.

I had just seen Ray Manzarek for the first time.

ROBBY KRIEGER

And, finally, there was Robby Krieger, The Doors' dexterous guitarist, the kid—he was the youngest of the group—who dazzled Jim Morrison with his bottleneck playing, and who grew up with rock 'n' roll, R&B, blues, jazz, and…flamenco!

I was born in Cedars of Lebanon Hospital, Los Angeles, California, 1946, 1 A.M., January 8. Same as Elvis. I had a twin brother, Ronnie, who had manic depression and died in 1985.

My dad, Stuart A. Krieger, was from Cleveland, Ohio. He went to Caltech and became an aeronautical engineer. He helped design the original Flying Wing. Remember in *War of the Worlds*, that plane they bomb the aliens with? That was a Flying Wing.

My mother, Marilyn, was a great lady. She was just a real smart person and I guess I got morals from her; she would never do anything that was shady or anything like that. I'm not saying my dad would, but she was just a very together person.

Neither of my parents was religious. Their parents were both Jewish, and they were brought up to be Jewish, and I think they both rebelled against that, and because of that my brother and I were never subjected to going to Sunday school or anything like that. We grew up in the Pacific Palisades, which is probably the most WASPy area of Los Angeles, and nobody knew we were Jewish.

My dad was always at work, and my mom, even though she was a wonderful person, she was hooked on pills a lot of the time. She had migraine headaches and stuff, and so she was in bed a lot of the time. So I had my reasons for being a bad kid, even though maybe I shouldn't have. Probably the worst thing was getting busted for pot at an early age. And the time when we broke into the high school while they were building it. It was right near where we lived. On Sundays we used to go over there, nobody around, here's all these beautiful tractors, and on one of them they left the key, and we had some nice drag races on that thing. Of course, the cops caught us and dragged us home.

We both turned out to be bad seeds, and got into trouble at University High, so we were sent away to different private schools. I went to Menlo School, which was a prep school for Stanford University. I was 16. And the funny thing was they took me out of public school to get rid of my unsavory friends, and my most unsavory friend ended up going there too. We actually didn't get into much trouble up there, except a couple of times drinking beer and stuff, but it really did straighten me out a bit. I became more mainstream, I guess you could say. It was cool being away from your parents. We got to go to San Francisco on weekends. That was where I really got into music. I used to go see Bob Dylan and Joan Baez and all kinds of great music.

And that's where I learned to play guitar. Bill Wolff—my "unsavory" friend from L.A.—had a guitar, and we played a lot, and I pretty quickly became the best guitar player up there. I got involved with the folk scene and played a few gigs with the official Bob Dylan neck-mounted harmonica. And Bill and I formed a jug band, the Back Bay Chamber Pot Terriers. Bob Weir had a jug band at the same time up there, and Jerry Garcia, they all had jug bands; that was the thing to do. Our first audience was the ladies' auxiliary at Menlo School.

I just always liked the guitar for some reason. When I was twelve years old, a friend of mine had a guitar and I was just drawn to it. I originally liked the trumpet, and wanted to play it so I could be the bugle guy at school. I took lessons, but I was no good at that. But that guitar—boy, that thing held the magic for me.

My first guitar was just a crummy nylon-string guitar, but I was interested in flamenco music and I had quite a few flamenco records, by Sabicas and Juan Serrano, so I decided that I wanted to play flamenco, and my friend Bill Wolff and I both decided we were going to learn flamenco. We took lessons from a couple of guys here in Hollywood.

And to play flamenco, you need a flamenco guitar. I mean you don't really, but it's better to have one because of the way it's set up; the strings are meant to buzz a little bit, especially the lower string. So the

There was also a lot of classical music in my house. In fact, the first music I heard that I liked was *Peter and the Wolf*. I think I was about seven. The first stuff that really caught my ear was at the YMCA, where on the jukebox they had "Rock Around the Clock." Boy, that thing just got played until the grooves wore out. Everybody played that song. And my mom always listened to the radio, and when I heard Elvis, and "Hound Dog," man, that was something else. That was unlike any music that I'd heard before. And then there was Little Richard and Fats Domino.

But Little Richard—man, that guy, for raw rock 'n' roll power, you can't beat him.

I had no idea what I was going to be. At Menlo School, all they cared about teaching you was how to pass the SAT test to get you into college, and I did. I got into UCSB, in Santa Barbara. Which was a big mistake. It was a total party school.

I was taking psychology. I figured that was the most innocuous of majors that you could pick, so no, I had no idea. But I did hope that I would be doing something in music after I learned how to play the guitar. I had taken flamenco lessons for maybe a year before, when I was home from school on summer vacation. So when I went to UCSB, I was giving flamenco lessons. But even then I didn't really think, "Oh, I'm going to be a guitar player for the rest of my life." For one thing, there was certainly no money in it. And it just seemed too far out of reality to actually bank on something like that.

And then I saw Chuck Berry at the Santa Monica Civic. He was incredible. That was the greatest Chuck Berry show I've ever seen because he was still young and not jaded or mad or something. He was really great that night and that did it for me. He had this red rockin' guitar. The next day, I went out and traded my classical in on a Gibson SG. I played that until it got ripped off, then got another. If I hadn't gone electric, I probably wouldn't have got into rock 'n' roll. Records got me into the blues, too—the newer kind of electric blues, like Paul Butterfield. I wanted to learn jazz, really, but I got to know some people who did rock with jazz, and I thought I could make some money playing music.

There was a band of hippies at UCSB. Longhairs few and far between at that point. We were doing acid and stuff, but there weren't a lot us, maybe twenty people that were hip, you know.

first flamenco guitar I got was actually a Mexican job; it was really a good guitar, it cost about $180 in those days, which was a lot. It was called a Ramirez, and Ramirez was actually a guitar builder in Spain, and I guess his brother had come over to Mexico and started building guitars down there. And then the next year, my dad happened to be going to Spain, and I said, "Dad, if you're in Madrid, can you please go to this place called Ramirez Guitars downtown and see if you can pick me up a flamenco guitar?" And he did, and I still have it to this day. A 1963 Ramirez flamenco guitar, and that's a real Ramirez. So I had the fake Ramirez first and then the real Ramirez.

My parents were very supportive. They were pretty much overjoyed that I would be interested in anything at that point, other than stealing stuff and setting stuff on fire.

At home, my dad had this amazing set of records, 78 rpms, rhythm and blues stuff that was unbelievable. It was like rock 'n' roll, but a little smoother, so it wasn't quite as exciting as rock 'n' roll, but it had the same changes and beat. I loved that stuff.

(below) Robby: "Playing my Sarod, à la Ali Akibar Khan. On my right is my sitar, and on my left is my Super 400 Gibson, my first free guitar, which I gave to our roadie, Vince Treanor."

The defining event in my life—besides hearing Bob Dylan do "Tambourine Man," that is—was when I first took a psychedelic drug. The first psychedelic drug I took was Morning Glory seeds. You buy them at the flower store and you grind them up and stick them in these huge horse capsules, and you just take as many as you can—twenty, thirty. Then you get a horrible stomach ache, and you throw up, and then you're stoned, and that really did change my life, man. I was a different person. It took you to a different place, I started speaking in an English accent at one point. And then that night I went to see Bob Dylan play at Long Beach, which was the first time he went rock 'n' roll, and I realized at that point, if I had been my normal self, I probably would have been real pissed off that he did that—oh, he's a folk guy, and now he's rock 'n' roll—but I zeroed in on it, and I dug it.

After determining that he was "getting nothing done whatsoever" at UC Santa Barbara, Krieger transferred to UCLA and moved back home. Before being sent to the prep school in Menlo Park, he had attended University High School in Los Angeles, where he met John Densmore. Krieger's budding interest in jazz and blues dovetailed nicely with Densmore's own musical tastes, and at UCLA they formed a band called the Psychedelic Rangers. The Rangers included Wolff and Densmore's buddy Grant Johnson, who played piano.

John: We took acid together, Robby, Grant, Bill, and I, and then we decided, "Well, let's form a band!" It was back when the word "psychedelic" wasn't really known. We were just screwing around, jamming on blues and a couple of originals.

Robby: We only had two originals, but we never really played gigs or anything; it was just a fun band. Let's see, what did we play? We probably did some Stones songs or something like that, just for fun, and we had a couple of songs of our own, the best one being a little thing called "Paranoia," written by myself and Grant.

At the same time, the inquisitive Krieger was beginning to explore Indian music.

Robby: I had a sitar and a sarod and took a lot of lessons on them. I even went to the Ravi Shankar School, which was called the Kinnara School. This was during Ravi Shankar's heyday. He had about ten teachers and millions of guys coming in with sitars.

And then, of course, there was the Meditation Center, where the psychedelic rangers, Robby and John, were seeking their bliss. In turn, they would be discovered, one after another, by Ray ("No bliss! No bliss!") Manzarek.

(below) The Doors & The Standells at Whittier High. Ray: "The Doors take a trip down Whittier Boulevard."

(below) Two L.A. legends meet when The Doors and The Byrds share a memorable early double-bill.

(below) "Cheetah" – Ray and Robby:
"An insane psychedelic ballroom where
Jim did his first stage dive. This was a
penance gig of sorts; we played this show
in trade for some radio attention from the
Humble Harv show on KHJ–AM radio."

2 ON THE BEACH

2 ON THE BEACH

Anne: When Jim started getting records in high school, the first one I remember was *Freewheelin'* by Bob Dylan. He loved Bob Dylan.

Jim: Y'see, the birth of rock 'n' roll coincided with my adolescence, my coming into awareness. It was a real turn-on, although at the time I could never allow myself to rationally fantasize about ever doing it myself.

At UCLA, Morrison had messed around some with a surf band called Rick and the Ravens, starring Rick and Jim Manzarek. At the end of a set, their brother, "Screamin' Ray Daniels, the bearded blues shouter" would join them for a few numbers, making good use of his classical piano lessons. The guys played venues like the Turkey Joint West in Santa Monica for a few bucks each on weekends. On occasion, Jim Morrison, who'd appeared briefly in a party scene in Induction, one of Manzarek's student films, would jump on stage to join in "Gloria" or "Louie Louie," and sing himself hoarse.

Ray: Rick and the Ravens had a gig backing up Sonny and Cher for a high school prom out at the Marina, and it's like two days before the gig, and my brother's sax player quits. My brother tells the booking guy, and the guy asks how many people are going to be there, and it was five. And the guy said, "Hey, I booked it for six, I'm paying for six, I want six people." So my brother says, "What will we do?" And I said, "I know what, we'll get Morrison." So I said to Jim, "Here's what you're going to do. You're going to wear a guitar, we turn it down to zero"—so he's onstage "playing." At the end of the night, after bopping around and posing like a guitar god, he made twenty bucks, and he said, "Ray, this is the easiest money I've ever made."

Jim: I never did any singing. I never even conceived it. I thought I was going to be a writer or a sociologist, maybe write plays. I never went to concerts—one or two at most. I saw a few things on TV, but I'd never been a part of it all.

I just got out of college. I wasn't doing much of anything. I was free for the first time. I had been going to school, constantly, for fifteen years … I wandered around; I was living down in the beach in abject poverty … It was a beautiful hot summer, and I just started hearing songs. I think I still have the notebook with those songs written in it.

But I heard in my head a whole concert situation, with a band and singing and an audience—a large audience. Those first five or six songs I wrote, I was just taking notes at a fantastic rock concert that was going on inside my head. And once I had written the songs, I had to sing them.

This kind of mythic concert that I heard … I'd like to try and reproduce it sometime, either in actuality or on record. I'd like to reproduce what I heard on the beach that day.

The beach was Venice, a small oceanside community that, at the turn of the twentieth century, had aspirations of becoming an upscale resort, with canals, beachfront homes, and shops. It never happened, and by the fifties, it was an attraction mainly to beatniks. In the mid-sixties, it was rundown and, as it

(below) The foursome walking into the great unknown. The Doors' original rehearsal space on Venice Beach is behind them on the right.

(left) The Doors on the Pacific, San
Francisco, 1967

was in the Haight-Ashbury up north, Venice, with its old housing, low rents, and cheap cafes—not to mention the Pacific Ocean—began to draw students, artists, hippies, and poor people. Ray Manzarek and his girlfriend, Dorothy, lived here in a one-bedroom apartment overlooking a garage.

Ray: It was probably after the Fourth of July weekend. I'm out on the beach and who comes walking along in the shore break but Jim Morrison. He was wearing cut-off shorts, no shirt, and no shoes and his feet were splashing the water as he walked. At UCLA, Jim was maybe 165, he was soft and no longer athletic; he used to be a swimmer. But now he must've weighed 135, 140. I thought, "Damn, he's lookin' good. This guy has abs."

He says, "Hey, Ray." I said, "Jim, come on over here, sit down with me." So he sits on my Indian bedspread. I said, "Hey man, what are you doing here? You back?" He said, "No, I never left. I've been up on Dennis Jakobs's rooftop here in Venice getting stoned and taking acid and writing songs." I said, "Far out, man, writing songs?" because I never realized Jim could write songs. I just knew he wrote poetry, and all of a sudden he became a songwriter.

I said, "You look great, man. How'd you lose all the weight?" He said, "Like I said, taking acid. And I don't eat." And he said, "I've been watching a rock concert in my mind and just sitting up there looking out on the beach and a rock concert's taking place and I'm the lead singer and these are my songs and I'm playing in a band." I said, "Well that's cool. What are the songs?" And he said, "Aw, I just…" And I said, "Come on man, sing me a song."

He said, "I don't know. I'm kind of shy and my voice isn't that good." I said, "Your voice isn't that good? Dylan is internationally famous with that squeaky voice of his. Come on." So he hops off the bedspread, digs both hands into the sand, and with the sand running out from between his fingers, closes his eyes, and starts singing "Moonlight Drive."

"Let's swim to the moon/Let's climb through the tide." He just sang the melody. "Penetrate the evening that the city sleeps to hide/Let's swim out tonight love/It's our turn to try/Parked beside the ocean on our moonlight drive." I said, "Whoa, wait a minute, man, I can really hear what I would do to that!" Just put it in a minor, dark, moody, funky, organ-y spacey kind of thing.

So that's how The Doors were born: Jim's lyrics and my moody music. He had great lyrics, and he was a poet. When he did "My Eyes Have Seen You," and then also "Summer's Almost Gone," I thought those songs lent themselves so beautifully to rock 'n' roll and chord changes that I could put on. "Summer's Almost Gone"—I could play Bach lines to it, and a sort of a slow Bolero kind of Latin jazz thing. "My Eyes Have Seen You" was a hot, uptempo Latin song, and "Moonlight Drive" was Jimmy Smith, Ray Charles, funky organ, just being cool and bluesy—*and* he had death in his lyrics! At the end of "Moonlight Drive," he says, "Come on, baby, gonna take a little ride, go down by the oceanside, get real close, get real tight, baby gonna drown tonight."

And I thought, *psychedelic,* because with LSD you realize that you are alive, but you're also occupying this bodily fleshy form that's going to deteriorate in seventy to eighty years. And Morrison was the first rock 'n' roller that I'd ever heard that brought death into the equation of youth; and I thought it was just brilliant.

Ray, I'm guessing, never sang "Tell Laura I Love Her" or "Teen Angel" with Rick and the Ravens. But, hey, he was probably talking about real rock 'n' roll.

Ray: Before Morrison, I had never seriously thought about rock 'n' roll. I was on the beach waiting to find out what the heck I was going to do with my life, thinking, "Is somebody going to allow me to make a film?" when Morrison came along and I heard those lyrics and I said, "This is it. To get a rock 'n' roll band together with a guy who was so amusing and so much fun and so knowledgeable and was writing original lyrics—I said, "Yeah, let's do it. Jim, we're gonna go all the way with this one!"

I said, "What do we call the band?" He said, "Oh, that's easy, man. The Doors."

As in William Blake's observation—"If the doors of perception were cleansed, everything would appear to man as it truly is, infinite"—and as in one of Morrison's favored books, *The Doors of Perception* by Aldous Huxley, all about his experiments with mescaline.

Morrison had mentioned the name a month or so before, when he was talking idly with a friend from FSU, Sam Kilman, who'd played drums as a kid. Out of nowhere, with a strange drawl and in a voice that indicated to pals that he might be joking, Jim told Sam that they should start a rock

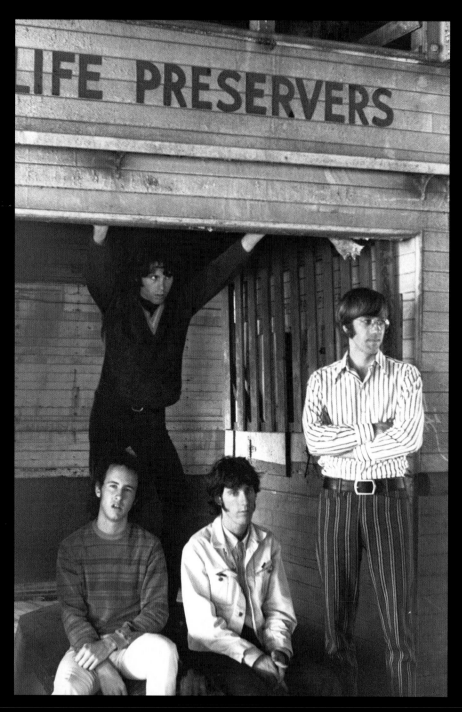

band, and that he could be the singer, even though he couldn't sing.
Kilman played along and asked what this band would be called.

"The Doors," Morrison replied readily. "There's the known. And there's
the unknown. And what separates the two is the door, and that's what I
want to be. *Ahh wanna be th' Dooooorrr…*"

"THIS IS NOT THE NEXT MICK JAGGER"

*Having lost Jim once before, Ray was not about to let Morrison's
songwriting discovery get away. They began to go to UCLA, where
they could sneak into practice rooms equipped with pianos, and work
up Morrison's songs. And Manzarek offered his former classmate a
slight upgrade from the rooftop in Venice: He could move in with him
and Dorothy.*

Ray: "Honey, Jim and I are getting a rock 'n' roll band together." And
she says, "Hmm." And she looked at Jim, looked at me, looked back at
Jim, nodded her head and said, "If you think it's good music…I'll tell
you, you guys got the look." We moved into the living room and let Jim
have the bedroom, because the living room had a heater, and he already
had an electric blanket. Dorothy always thought he was a rich kid.

Now, this is the other part of the magical meeting of The Doors. I met
John at this Maharishi meditation thing. Somebody said that John was
a drummer, and I went to John and I say, "I've got a singer and I play
keyboards and we're gonna get a rock 'n' roll band together. Wanna
join?" And John said, "Yeah, I'll come down and see how it sounds."

John: I met Jim at Ray's garage. He had never sung, and he just started
singing. It wasn't as full as on record, but it was just total confidence, like,
"Oh, I'm gonna be a singer." Nothing about singing from the diaphragm
or however you're supposed to. He just sang or yelled or whatever he
was doing. But I guess he was doing it right; he just was a natural. He
was so shy, I thought, "This is not the next Mick Jagger."

In the pre-Robby stages of The Doors, we rehearsed in Manzarek's
parents' garage in Manhattan Beach. I remember thinking Manzarek's
brothers were cool musicians. They were playing blues and that was OK
with me. I had an attitude 'cause I was a jazz musician.

Jim wore brown cords, a T-shirt, and he never seemed to wear shoes. Ray had a daisy in his shirt and Rick had real long hair, like someone in the Grateful Dead, which I thought was tacky 'cause we were more modeling ourselves after the early Stones, who had pretty cool clothes. We had this confidence about us that when we were rehearsing, before we even played a club, we just were gonna do it. We just knew we had some special chemistry.

But not enough. Not, at least, in the "pre-Robby stages."

Jim: Rick and the Ravens had a contract with World Pacific. They'd tried to get a couple of singles out, but nothing happened. They still had a contract to do a few sides, and we'd gotten together by then, so we went in and cut six sides in about three hours. At that time, Robby wasn't in the band, but John was. He was drumming, Ray was on piano, I was singing, and Ray's two brothers played harp and guitar … and there was a girl bass player—I can't remember her name.

Neither can anyone else. But, that day in September 1965, at the label's studio in downtown Los Angeles, the group went through the Morrison songbook, such as it was: "Moonlight Drive," "Hello, I Love You," "My Eyes Have Seen You," "Summer's Gone," "End of the Night," and "Go Insane."

Especially compared with what Jim, John, and Ray would do a little more than a year later, the demo was rough. The sound was hollow— on "Go Insane," Ray plinked a keyboard that sounded like a toy piano. The arrangements were pedestrian; the tempo of "Moonlight Drive" recalled the R&B hit "Hully Gully." But the lyrics—Manzarek was right. Morrison was writing like no other.

At one label after another, the demo was rejected. At Capitol, the receptionist wouldn't set up a meeting with an A&R person. At Dunhill Records, where producer Lou Adler was riding high on Barry McGuire's "Eve of Destruction" and grooming The Mamas & the Papas, Adler dropped the needle of his turntable on one track after another, giving each about ten seconds before declaring that he'd heard nothing he could use. Jim Morrison then told Adler, with derision: "That's all right. We don't want to be used, anyway."

(left) Ray, Robby, John, and Jim,
showing why the ladies loved him,
Venice Beach, 1967

Jim: I took the demos everywhere I could possibly think, just going in the door and telling the secretary what I wanted. Sometimes they'd say, "Leave your number," sometimes they'd let you talk to someone else. The reception game. At Columbia, they became interested.

The friendly ear at Columbia Records belonged to Billy James.

Billy James: I had the "company freak" job. I was a manager of talent acquisition and development. Morrison said he'd seen my picture in a trade magazine and liked my beard.

I signed them after hearing their demo. I came back from lunch one day and there they were.

I was tantalized. They seemed to be playing at playing. There seemed to be an aloofness from the material, almost parody. And I'm a sucker for that. The demo made it clear they had an unusual concept.

I signed them to a contract for six months, and within that six months, Columbia had to release two or four sides, or lose them.

As it turned out, it had taken only a month or so before the band found a taker. But youth is impatient, and while they awaited further word from the record company, the group fell apart, as Ray's two brothers decided to try other lines of work. The band suddenly had a job opening or two.

CHAMPAGNE BLUES

Ray: It was late fall, early winter 1965. They said, this is not happening. They were right; it wasn't happening. So my brothers said listen, you guys go, do whatever you want, but we're gonna move on and do something else.

So now we needed a guitar player. We auditioned a guy, Bill Wolff, a friend of John's and Robby's, but he was really fast and it wasn't quite what we were looking for. Well, after another meditation class or two, John Densmore said, "Hey, you see that guy over there? That's Robby Krieger." They had played together in a band with Wolff. I never asked

John and Robby why they were at the meditation, and it didn't matter. It's like the great Mick Jagger line, "You can't always get what you want, but if you try sometimes you get what you need."

Robby: So, John brought Jim over to my house one night and I happened to have the slide guitar out and played a few notes, and he flipped for it. Jim said, "That's it; he's got to be in the group."

Ray: Robby comes to a rehearsal and we go to my friend Hank Olguin's house. Hank was in one of my student movies, and he had a house in Santa Monica, with a piano.

So Morrison has a little amplifier and a microphone and a stand, and he's gonna sing through the amplifier, I'm gonna play Hank's piano, and John brings his drums.

And Robby comes in with his amp and his Gibson guitar and plugs it in and I show him the chord changes and how "Moonlight Drive" goes, kind of dark and spooky, and Robby opens his guitar case and pulls out a bottleneck. Robby slips it on his finger and he hits the low E string and goes *beooww, beeeee, beeoowww,* and it was like glass on steel, and it sounded like a sitar. Morrison says, "That's the sound; that's the sound." And we begin to play the song. And he couldn't contain himself. Jim said, "I want that sound on every single song!" I said, "On every song? Don't you think that's a bit much?" "Well," he said, "maybe not every song, but a lot of them."

Robby: I had the blues records of the day and was fooling around with it. I hadn't heard anybody do it on electric guitar, so that was what I was trying to do: incorporate the bottleneck with the electric guitar.

John: Bottleneck had been used acoustically in folk music, and with blues singers.

Robby: I was the first to do it out of the blues genre. Brian Jones did do it on "Little Red Rooster," a blues song.

Krieger's favorite homemade bottlenecks came from champagne bottles, he said. He favored their longish necks.

Ray: So we smoked a joint, passed the peace pipe around, and we began to play "Moonlight Drive."

John: We were doing "Moonlight Drive," and I thought, "This is unique, man, these liquid electric poetic lyrics, and there's something here— there really *is* something here—and Jim is so smart and great looking and crazy: dangerous. That's worrisome. I mean, I knew he was a little different from the beginning.

Robby: Everything just clicked. Jim was great. But then a weird thing happened at the end of that rehearsal. This guy came in, he and Jim went to the back of the room, he and Jim had words, and Jim went crazy on the guy. It turned out to be a dope deal gone bad. Jim was very upset.

The next rehearsal, however, turned out to be a bust. We decided to do it at my parents' house in Pacific Palisades. Ray and John came over; John brought all his drums. No Jim. He and some friends had taken a road trip to Blythe. They got into a fight with some bikers and got arrested. That was my introduction to Jim being late to the rehearsals. I thought, oh my God, this is the second rehearsal. Where is it going to go from here? And it did go downhill.

So we started rehearsing at Ray's place. It was in Venice on the strand, somewhere between Washington and the Marina. It was a great place, a California shingled beach house with big blue-, green-, and white-tinted bay windows overlooking the sand, with dark wood. It was $200 a month. Two hundred dollars a month was not cheap in those days and somehow Ray finagled us all into chipping in even though he was the one living there. We did get back at Ray in other ways for making us pay. Jim and I would get drunk and get some girls and go over there in the morning. I remember one time I had a girl over there and Ray caught me in the bedroom. What could he say? I was paying the rent.

John: There used to be crumbling Victorian beach houses or California Craftsman shingled houses, and you could rent these ten-room mansions for a few hundred bucks, so we did. The boardwalk was empty, completely stark except for a few straggling beatniks from the Gaslight, where Allen Ginsberg used to read, and a few old Hasidic

Jews in front of the temple. It was so deserted, I used to think if I'm poor I'm gonna live here, 'cause this is so cool, and no one's around.

The main room was pretty empty except for our equipment, and LPs laying around on the wood floors: Jimmy Reed, John Lee Hooker, Muddy Waters, early Dylan, Bertolt Brecht's *Mahogany* opera, and tons of jazz, like Miles Davis and John Coltrane. Ray and I really connected over our mutual love of jazz.

Ray: I'd played music practically my entire life. But the first time I ever *really* played music was with John and Robby and Jim. We played "Moonlight Drive" and a couple of other songs after getting stoned down by the beach. That's where it happened. It was an epiphany, a moment of profound clarity. That first time, *boom,* just like that. I thought, "Wow, that's the greatest musical experience I've ever had in my whole life."

John: There was ample herb going around and when we would break for lunch we would sit out on the beach between rehearsals and look at the planes taking off from LAX. I thought, "Someday we'll be on one of those. We'll go east and conquer the Occidental." I was eighteen years old and I had never even been on a plane.

We had many daydreams. I used to drive Jim, who didn't have a car, to the Sunset Strip and we would stand at night outside the Whisky and dream of playing.

From the beginning, The Doors sounded like no other band. Truly. To begin with, they had no interest in sounding like anyone else. And technically, they could not have replicated any other rock band. First, they had no success finding a suitable bass player, so Manzarek assigned his left hand that job. And that was fine by Densmore.

John: So we didn't have a bass player—that's why I got to really get in there as a drummer and play around, because there was much more room. When we made albums, we always had a bass player, because you have to have that punch on a record. But in person Ray played a keyboard bass, so there was some mushy bottom, that's about all, but

(below) Ray: "The entire glassed-in room was ours. We set up the Vox Continental, the Fender Rhodes keyboard bass, John's Mod Orange drum set, Robby's amp, and Jim's vocal mike. The result? 'Light My Fire.'"

there was lots of room to fill and crash around. After a while, I just let it go, played around with what Jim's doing, let it go, and it got psychedelic.

You had a guitarist who was playing world music a decade or two before that term was coined, playing flamenco, Indian ragas, folk, bottlenecked blues, and rock. And the lead singer?

Adm. Morrison: I just don't think he'll ever be a Caruso or be famous particularly for his voice. But he was more than a voice; he was an entertainer. There's something there that's hard to describe; it was the relationship he managed to establish with an audience ... that made him a success.

Andy: I don't think you can put his voice in the same league with Elvis and Frank Sinatra and some of the other greats. I'm with my dad. But I'm not a professional musician, either. I'd be interested to see what a real professional who studies voice would say.

Paul Rothchild: Jim was blessed with a magnificent vocal instrument. His was one of the greatest voices I've ever had the delight to work with. He talked about being a crooner. He admired Sinatra's phrasing enormously. And he could do a great Elvis. But he was really an accidental musician. He couldn't play an instrument.

Rothchild, by the way, also told the writer Eve Babitz, "Jim was the greatest crooner since Bing Crosby." Unlike **Der Bingle,** *Jim was also a fan of LSD, and he had never sung before, but had a knack for writing poetry as rock lyrics.*

Still, as amazing and varied as those first songs of Morrison's were, they amounted to only eight or ten numbers. After several rehearsals, Jim gave his bandmates some homework at the end of one session in December 1965:

Robby: Jim said, "Hey, guys, we don't have enough original songs. Why don't you try writing?" That was just before a weekend, and within a few days, I wrote "Light My Fire."

I would say that—and "Love Me Two Times" were the first real total songs that I wrote. I don't remember whether the words came first ... I

(below) "Under Surveillance" – The FBI agent on the right seems suspiciously close to the guys as they visit a San Francisco bookstore, 1967

think the music did. I was trying to come up with something that was reminiscent of "Hey Joe," the version by The Leaves.

Actually, Krieger didn't quite have a total song. As he and the band worked out the arrangement, they discovered that the song had only a first verse and chorus.

Ray: Jim came up with lyrics for the second verse:

The time to hesitate is through
No time to wallow in the mire
Try now, we can only lose
And our love becomes a funeral pyre

Manzarek added the crowning touch. Believing that the song needed an instrumental introduction, he sent the three others outside to the beach while he worked at his keyboard.

Ray: All my classical studies came to fruition. A simple circle of fifths was the answer. The chords were G to D, F to Bb, Eb to Ab (two beats on each chord), and then an A for two measures. Run some Bach filigrees over the top in a turning-in-on-itself Fibonacci spiral—like a nautilus shell—and you've got it. "Eureka!"

I called the guys back. "I got it," I said. "Check this out. I'll count it off. John, give me a snare shot on four. Robby, just listen and come in on the A minor. Jim, sing where you're supposed to. Ready?" I was speeding. Sweet creativity, what a transcendent state.

1…2…1-2-3, *CRACK!* John shot me with his snare and we were off. Cartwheeling into "Light My Fire."

Robby: And then, when we started playing "Light My Fire" live and people would go nuts over it, we knew, "OK, that's probably a hit record right there."

If only they could make a record, or get some kind of work.

(below) "Love That Mexican Food" – The rest of the band is oblivious as Jim plays to the camera at the band's favorite hangout, the Lucky U Cafe, 1967

(below) The Venice canals, 1967

(right) Sausalito, CA, 1967

3 THE MEN IN THE FOG

3 THE MEN IN THE FOG

The Doors had a contract with Columbia Records, but they didn't have any of the most vital tools of the trade: a manager, an agent, a publicist. Their first gigs, then, were frat parties, friends' bashes, a wedding or two, and even a frigid boat ride in November of 1965. Just before Christmas, they played at their alma mater, UCLA, providing an acoustic backdrop for one of Ray's films in the film school's presentation of the best student films of the year.

All this time, they were still thinking about what was happening a few miles east, in West Hollywood, on that patch of Sunset Boulevard known around the world as the Sunset Strip. Robby said they knocked on the door of every club in all the back alleys of Hollywood.

Ray: And we get rejected at Bido Lido's and rejected here and there, but finally we get the audition at the London Fog on the Sunset Strip, down the street from the Whisky a Go Go. Whisky a Go Go is mecca. Outside of I guess the Cavern Club the Whisky a Go Go was the greatest nightclub on earth at that particular time.

So we auditioned just down the street from the Whisky a Go Go, at a place called the London Fog. We went in there one or two times before the audition and it was pretty dead; the place was always empty.

And we asked if we could audition. The guy said, "Yeah, come by next Monday night." And Jim said, "You know what we got to do. This place is dead; we've got to fill this place with our friends for our audition."

So we contact everybody we know at UCLA. John and Robby contact their friends.

Sure enough, that Monday night we set our equipment up in a strange little club, and we're up on sort of a pedestal with our heads—Jim virtually was about an inch from hitting his head on this low ceiling. It was an odd place to play.

Robby: Well, the London Fog was really a nothing. It was a dump. It was just a last resort place where you played to try to make five bucks a night. I don't even remember who played there of any note other than us. It was sort of a gay bar as far as I know. I don't think they even had live music before us because the stage was like not even a stage, it was this kind of a platform—it was really a go-go platform is what it was 'cause we could barely fit up there. We didn't have much gear, either.

Ray: And some people start drifting in, and we start playing, and then more and more of our friends start drifting in, so that by ten o'clock the place was packed with people, and they're drinking beers and ordering and the owner of the place, Jesse James—what a perfect name, the bandit of the Sunset Strip—was in ecstasy, because it just worked out that as we were playing, people were coming in. So he thought, these guys are drawing people in. It wasn't like a packed place waiting to see us. He would have been able to see through that. And at the end of the set, Jesse James said, "This is amazing, this place has never been so packed on a Monday night. This is incredible man. You guys got the gig."

3 THE MEN IN THE FOG

(below) The Doors hone their sound at
Ondine in New York City, 1966

It was February 1966. The night after the audition, the Fog was back to its usual, empty state. Besides a puzzled Jesse James, there was a bartender, the loyal Dorothy Fujikawa, a hooker or two, a sailor or three, and Rhonda Lane, the house go-go dancer.

Ray: There was, like, never more than ten, fifteen people in the place at one time, Friday and Saturday nights included. It was pathetic. But Morrison was developing his voice and developing his strength and everything, and the idea that he was shy, I think that comes from Jim looking at us, not that he was afraid to face the audience. There *was* no audience for him to face.

Now, when you rehearse, you face each other. Everybody faces each other. You're not set up with the lead singer looking out at a blank wall with the band behind him. Invariably you play in a circle when you're rehearsing. And that's what we did onstage.

By the end of playing at that London Fog, *we were good.*

It took that time at the London Fog, in other words, for Morrison, who'd reminded Manzarek early on of the jazz musician Chet Baker, with his soft voice, to begin to project, to perform.

John: Precisely. And at the London Fog he literally turned it around, you know, got the nerve to face the audience and developed his own thing.

Now that they were professional performers, The Doors began to put together their onstage look. Or not. They were a motley crew. Krieger and Densmore's outfits were flower-powered; Manzarek, the elder, was preppy, with Ivy League sport coats and slacks. Morrison, before he discovered—or could afford—black leather, seemed content with getting his clothes at Goodwill Industries.

Ray: At UCLA, he wore hospital outfits—a hospital shirt and chuka boots and chinos. He didn't wear denim or Levi's.

And now that they were making some money—if you could call five dollars a night "money"—they began to work out a business plan of sorts.

In his Elektra bio, Morrison noted, after some musings about astrology: "...the main thing is that we are The Doors." By that, he meant that they were a band, a team of equal members. For example, it was Robby who came up with "Light My Fire." Jim helped with a verse; Ray composed the intro; John set the beat. So why not credit the song to the entire band, and split all royalties equally? "Jim said, 'We'll never fight. Let's make it a four-way split.'" The same, of course, would apply to songs that Morrison had written, which, as it turned out, would account for a large part of the band's output.

In spring, The Doors continued to play to handsful of paying customers at the London Fog.

It would have helped if they could make something of their recording deal. But, on an impromptu visit to Billy James, The Doors discovered that the label was planning to drop them.

Billy James: There were three or four producers on the West Coast for Columbia Records, and each of them just couldn't make room for a group I had signed. It's the large-company syndrome.

Morrison was incensed.

Ray: And Jim said, "Well, fine, just give us our release." And Billy said, "Don't take a release. If you wait two more months, you'll get a thousand dollars." And Jim said, "No, we'll be free right now. Just give us the release." "Wouldn't you like a thousand dollars?" No shit. Yeah, we'd like a thousand dollars; that would be like five months rent on the rehearsal place. But Jim said, "You don't want us; we don't want to be here. Just let us go. Give us our release right here and right now." So there goes our deal with Columbia Records.

They retreated, glumly, to the London Fog, where, all around them, things were heating up.

Jac Holzman: The time was the summer of 1966, and the place was the Sunset Strip, which had suddenly morphed before everyone's astonished eyes into the hippie navel of the universe.

Ray: People who had let their hair grow long, people who saw The Beatles and The Stones and the English invasion and thought that was definitely the way to look. And the Strip was a safe haven for that kind of person: the freaks, the outsiders, the different people.

Robby: Every night in the summertime it was just one big street scene. Cars lined up bumper to bumper. We hit all the clubs. The Sea Witch, an underground kind of place. Pandora's Box, the Unicorn, the Trip, the Galaxy, next to the Whisky, Brave New World, and Bido Lito's.

THE FIRST WHISKY BAR

Of all the Sunset Strip spots, it was the Whisky a Go Go that was action central. Elmer Valentine, one of the owners of another club, P.J.'s, visited Paris in 1963 and visited a hotspot called "Whisky a Go Go." A disc jockey played records, and people danced all night. The locals called the club a "discotheque."

Valentine and a couple of partners took over a club on Sunset Boulevard called the Party, which, in its previous incarnation, was a branch of the Bank of America.

To perform at his new club, Valentine poached Johnny Rivers from a nearby restaurant, Gazzari's. Rivers, who was from New York by way of Baton Rouge, played guitar and performed uptempo covers of pop and R&B songs—perfect for dancing.

On the evening of January 15, 1964, a who's who of Hollywood helped pack the Whisky a Go Go (the "e" in whiskey had to be dropped, to avoid the appearance of promoting, banish the thought, an alcoholic drink). After a DJ had played a set, Rivers and his band climbed onstage, tore into "Johnny B. Goode," people flocked to the floor to do the Watusi and the Frug, and the club became an instant institution.

January 15 was also just about the time, as it happens, that Jim Morrison arrived in Los Angeles, transferring from Florida State to UCLA.

But by 1966, rock 'n' roll was beginning to experience a seismic shift. Led by The Beatles, The Rolling Stones, Bob Dylan, and an emerging folk-rock scene ignited by Dylan, rock was getting…serious, with social and political messages. It still swung; it still rocked. But now, the World War II baby boomers began questioning a war in Southeast Asia, the history of segregation in the South, and, in short, the status quo. They were discovering and experimenting with drugs. Now, pop music began moving minds as well as bodies.

At the Whisky, Elmer Valentine and company—no fools, they—changed with the times and began booking a new generation of rock bands: local, national, international. Out went the Watusi; in came Buffalo Springfield, The Chambers Brothers, The Animals, and Jimi Hendrix.

Meantime, down the block, at the London Fog, The Doors were about to be let go, as Jesse James tired of the emptiness all around. Just before he terminated The Doors, however, Ronnie Harran, who helped book the bands for the Whisky, dropped in, caught sight of Morrison, and was hooked. She soon offered The Doors a gig as the Whisky's house band, opening for its various star acts.

At that point, The Doors had only a dozen or so songs, plus R&B and blues classics. They may have been able to repeat themselves endlessly at the Fog, since no one was listening. But for two sets a night at the Whisky, they needed to expand its act.

Ray: Repeat and stretch. "Light My Fire" took off into solos. "The End" became the epic we know now.

Elmer Valentine: Lots of groups want to do a twenty- or thirty-minute set. When The Doors played here, they wanted to play. I literally had to get the hook to get them off.

Although it's been written that The Doors opened for Them, with Van Morrison, on their very first night as the house band, that's not true. They auditioned and were officially hired early in May, and started work on the twenty-third, opening for Captain Beefheart, Buffalo Springfield, and Love before Them hit town for a two-week run beginning June 2. On their last night, Them are joined onstage by The Doors, and they jam on Wilson Pickett's "In the Midnight Hour" and an extended version of a Them song that The Doors had been playing since their early, lonely nights at the London Fog: "Gloria."

Ray: Van Morrison was insane…the guy was all over the stage, man. Did that thing of holding the microphone upside down and singing, and smashing the microphone stand into the ground and just…god, was he incredible! He was so good. Then the last night we had a jam.

John: Two Morrisons, two guitars, two drums, two keyboards. The Doors meet Them.

Elmer: I didn't like him at first. He was ahead of his time on certain things—like swearing.

But he had a kind of magic. The Doors were just the second group, but those calls kept coming in. "When's that horny motherfucker coming back?" The phones were unbelievable. You knew they were going to be stars.

Jac Holzman: In May of 1966, I had flown to L.A. and was picked up at the airport by Ronnie Harran. Arthur Lee was playing the Whisky and expected me to drop by. It was 11 P.M. L.A. time, 2 A.M. New York–

3 THE MEN IN THE FOG

(below and right) A great rock 'n' roll
moment when two Morrisons—Van and
Jim—unite on "Gloria," the Whisky, 1966

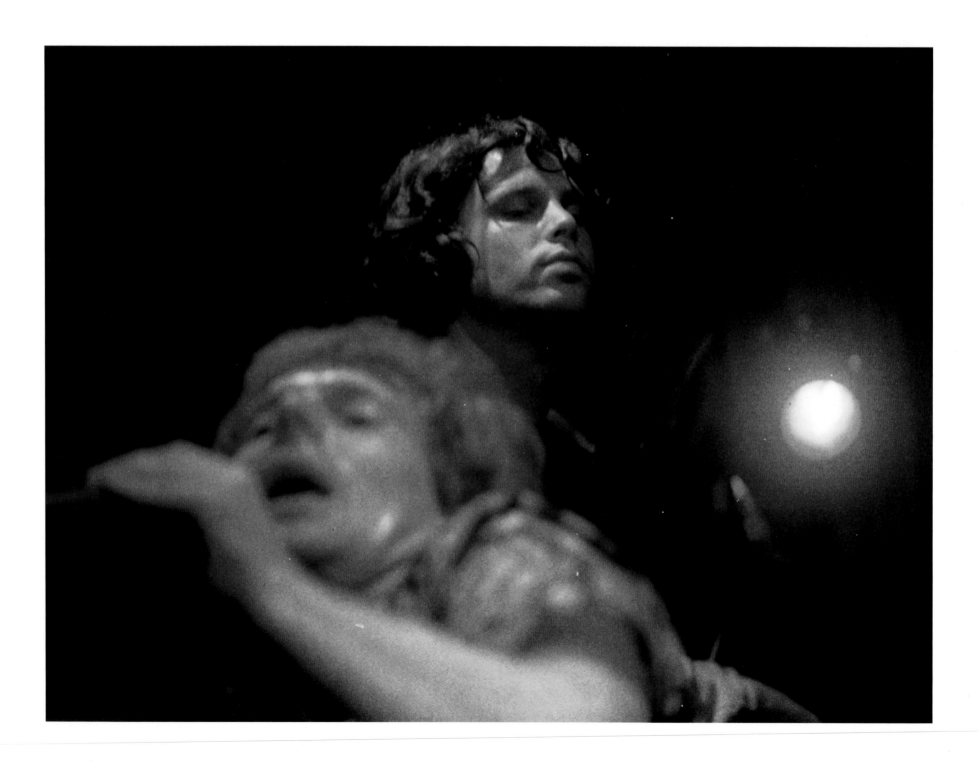

metabolism time. I was beat, but I went. Arthur urged me to stick around for the next band. Whoever they were, Arthur had a high opinion of them, and I had a very high opinion of Arthur's opinion, so I stayed.

It was The Doors, and they did nothing for me. Jim was lovely to look at, but there was no command. Perhaps I was thinking too conventionally, but their music had none of the rococo ornamentation with which a lot of rock 'n' roll was being embellished—remember, this was still the era of The Beatles and "Revolver," circa 1966. Yet, some inner voice whispered that there was more to them than I was seeing or hearing, so I kept returning to the club.

Finally, the fourth evening, I heard them. Jim generated an enormous tension with his performance, like a black hole, sucking the energy of the room into himself. The bass line was Ray Manzarek playing a second keyboard—piano bass—an unusual sound, very cadenced and clean. On top of Ray, Robby Krieger laid shimmering guitar. And John Densmore was the best drummer imaginable for Jim—whatever Morrison did, Densmore could follow with his jazz drummer's improvisational skill and sensitivity. They weren't consistent and they needed some fine-tuning before they would be ready to record, but this was no ordinary rock 'n' roll band.

Ray: And he came back the next time and, fortunately, that set we played "Alabama Song (The Whisky Bar)" by Bertolt Brecht and Kurt Weill. Dorothy Fujikawa had the record, and she said, "Why don't you guys do 'The Whisky Bar'?" And Jim said, "Dorothy, good idea."

So that night we happen to play a 1929 German opera song, and I think that pushed it over the edge. Jac Holzman went, "Oh, these boys are intelligent."

Jac: Kurt Weill's "Alabama Song" was a surprise coming from a rock band, and their arrangement impressed me. And when I heard, really heard, Manzarek's baroque organ line under "Light My Fire," I was ready to sign them.

Holzman summoned Paul Rothchild, one of Elektra's favored producers, to fly out from New York to see The Doors, and to give him and his wife Nina an additional opinion.

3 THE MEN IN THE FOG

Paul: We saw the first set. I thought to myself, "My God, Jac and Nina have lost their minds. These guys *suck!*"

At the same time they were awful, I could tell they were very different from anything I'd heard before. They were totally unique. That's usually a signal that someone is either fucking *terrible* or on the verge of brilliance. This intrigued me, so I stayed for the second set. Well, they were still rough around the edges, but they were brilliant. I turned 180 degrees in my thinking about the group.

They were a bunch of amateur musicians having a good time. It was *very* dramatic. In that second set I heard "The End," "Light My Fire," "Twentieth Century Fox," "Break On Through," and a few others, and I was convinced. Elektra signed them shortly after that.

Ray: All right! We just started jumping up and down. Elektra was a very hip label from New York.

Robby: Koerner, Ray & Glover being on Elektra—when I was in high school they were my idols, that band and that label. To be on Elektra was the greatest thing.

Jac: I offered what was slightly on the generous side of a standard deal in 1966 for an unproven group. Elektra would advance all recording costs plus $5,000 cash to the band against a five percent royalty with a separate advance against publishing, of which The Doors would own seventy-five percent and we would own twenty-five. And as a show of faith, I committed to release three albums.

Ray: Jac wasn't offering much money. But a guarantee to record and release three albums—that was fabulous. We could create anything we wanted to, and Elektra would put it out. We had material for two albums. So we knew that all the songs we had would be recorded, and the records would be in record stores, and we also had a guarantee of doing another record on top of that. So we felt incredibly secure.

Jac was fabulous that way: "We're signing you, because we want you to be creative." In effect, Jac Holzman to The Doors was like Diaghilev to Nijinsky and Stravinsky. It had all gotten rather anticlimactic at the Whisky because we had gotten our recording contract. That was the important thing—to make records—and we had been playing there for quite a while. So Jim was getting a little lackadaisical about some of his performances. One night...

It was August 21, 1966...

Robby: Jim is late.

Ray: We expect him to walk onstage any moment, and he doesn't. We play a whole first set without him. The headliners come on, and Phil Tanzini, one of the owners, grabs me and says, "You better get that Morrison boy. I got a contract here for four performers."

Robby: We were in trouble.

Ray: Maybe he's passed out in his room, maybe he's asleep. John and I go over to the Tropicana and pound on the door of his room. We hear a little scurrying around inside. "Hey, Jim, it's John, it's Ray. Come on, open up."

The door knob turns, very slowly, and the door opens, and there is Jim Morrison standing in his underwear and his boots, with his eyes blazing. Totally zonked out. We looked at him and said, "Oh my God, what are you on?"

Long story shorter: He's on LSD. Still, the show—or at least the second set at the Whisky—must go on, and Ray and John manage to get him there.

Ray: We start to play, and Jim is sort of half there, half not there. Some of the songs he's singing, some he's mumbling, he's standing with his back to the audience, and the crowd is getting slightly restless. Then he wants to do "The End." The club is filled; people are drinking and dancing. "The End" closes the set, and Jim wants to do it in the middle of the second set.

Robby: It was his favorite song on acid.

Ray: So we started to play it. And we never played it so brilliantly. It just became more and more hypnotic.

3 THE MEN IN THE FOG

(below) The band's home away from home, the Whisky a Go Go, 1966

We got to the middle of the song and there's an improvisational area where Jim could do anything he wanted. We're playing very softly, just keeping the vamp going, waiting for him to come in. And he begins.

"The killer awoke before dawn…He put his boots on…He took a face from the ancient gallery…And he walked on down the hallway."

It froze the Whisky. I looked out at the audience and I could see that nobody was dancing. The waitresses had stopped taking drink orders. Even the dancers…

John: Bell-bottoms stopped flapping. And he'd never done that part: "The killer woke before dawn…"

Ray: He tells the story of the killer going down the hallway, his family, and finally—he gets to "Father, I want to kill you!" and "Mother…I WANT TO FUCK YOU!"

Jim: Oedipus is a Greek myth. Sophocles wrote about it. I don't know who before that. It's about a man who inadvertently killed his father and married his mother. Yeah, I'd say there was a similarity, definitely. But to tell you the truth, every time I hear that song, it means something else to me. I really don't know what I was trying to say. It just started out as a simple good-bye song. Probably just to a girl, but I could see how it could be good-bye to a kind of childhood. I really don't know. I think it's sufficiently complex and universal in its imagery that it could be almost anything you want it to be.

Anne: He liked bringing ancient Greek stuff to life in a modern way, like a playwright would do. There's always the Oedipal thing redone, and I think he enjoyed that.

Ray: *Oedipus Rex*, right? He was giving voice in a rock 'n' roll setting to the Oedipus complex, at the time a widely discussed tendency in Freudian psychology. He wasn't saying he wanted to do that to his own mom and dad. He was reenacting a bit of Greek drama. It was theatre! It was all make-believe. (Or was it?)

(left) The Whisky, 1966

(below) Jim surrenders to the spirit onstage at the Whisky, 1966

But Phil Tanzini, co-owner of the Whisky, along with Elmer Valentine and Mario Maglieri, certainly didn't think it was playacting. It was real to him and it was verboten! He charged into our dressing room. "You filthy motherfuckers," he shrieked. He was hysterical. "You guys are all sick. This is the sickest band I've ever heard." He swept the room, pointing at each of us. "You're all fucked…too much pot! You goddamned fuckin' hippies."

"We're not hippies," Jim protested. "We're artists." Phil wheeled about, nostrils flaring, snorting.

"You are the sickest of the bunch, Morrison!" He was apoplectic. "You can't say that about your mother, you asshole. You filthy fucking, sick motherfucking asshole son of a bitch! You can't say that! About your mother?!"

Veins popping in his neck and forehead. Steaming, enraged. "You're fired! You shit. You finish up this week…and you're fucking fired! You understand me?!"

"Sure, Phil," Jim said. "But … do we still have a bar tab?"

Jim: "The End" is about three things: sex, death, travel…the theme is the same as in "Light My Fire," liberation from the cycle of birth-orgasm-death.

If you want to, take "The End" as being about patricide and incest. Read the last note to mean accommodation, not extermination, if that suits you more. That's as twentieth-century as you can get. I only aim to please.

(below left) Jim at the Whisky, 1966

(following page) Worlds collide when The Doors and Them jam on "Gloria," Whisky a Go Go, 1966

4 BREAK ON THROUGH

4 BREAK ON THROUGH

Just as The Doors had blithely bounced from the London Fog up the street to the Whisky, so they shook off their firing from the Whisky and prepared to make their first album. They didn't have a manager or an attorney, so Robby's father, Stu, brought in his own lawyer, a seasoned Beverly Hills attorney named Max Fink. He helped hammer out their Elektra deal, and soon The Doors were at their new job, as Elektra recording artists. They convened at Sunset Sound Studios, a little over a mile east of the Whisky, and met with the producer, Paul Rothchild, along with a young engineer named Bruce Botnick, who came with Sunset Sound.

Rothchild, at thirty, was eight years older than Jim Morrison. By sixties standards, he was an old guy, not to be trusted. But he had coproduced, with Mark Abramson, Paul Butterfield Blues Band's East–West *album for Elektra.*

Robby: We loved that record. Plus, the guy had just gotten out of jail, so we figured he couldn't be all bad.

Rothchild had recently served eight months for possession of a too-large amount of marijuana. In other words, he was a producer with a real record.

John: It took only six days to record because we had worked on these songs for nearly a year. Paul had recently gotten out of jail on a dope bust and Jac Holzman was giving him a break. Rothchild had produced Paul Butterfield, which impressed us. Doing time also appealed to our rebel nature.

Robby: The first night, we were afraid to play too loud. With all that expensive equipment in there, we were afraid that we'd blow it out.

In these days of technological marvels, when musicians can record on forty-eight or more tracks, it's all the more remarkable that The Doors sounded as accomplished as they did on that first album, using a four-track tape machine—and not even using all four tracks, at that.

Paul: And up until about a year before that, I'd been doing everything two-track. Actually, though, most of the first album is three-track. We'd put bass and drums on one track, guitar and organ on another, and Jim's vocals on the third. We used the fourth track for a few overdubbing things. Like on "Twentieth Century Fox" [written by Morrison, with music by Krieger] I got the whole band out onto a wooden platform and made them march. If you listen to the rhythm sound on the chorus, it sounds like a small German army! I'd just done a flamenco record where I'd used a similar idea. I thought it would be great to put it on a rock 'n' roll record.

We also overdubbed Morrison singing harmony to himself on a couple of things. Double-voicing was a thing to do. It was avant garde. Overdubbing harmony certainly wasn't new, but the idea of doubling a voice was still considered radical. It was as new then as digital delay is now.

(previous spread) The Doors in the recording studio with their production team, Bruce Botnick and Paul A. Rothchild

(below) Working out a tune in the studio during the *Waiting for the Sun* sessions with producer Paul Rothchild (center). Doug Lubahn, studio bass player, is at left, rear.

Things were wonderful in the sixties because it was an era of intense experimentation. Everyone was trying to out-hip each other. With The Doors, we tried to strike a very fine line between being very fresh and original and being documentary—making the record sound like it really happened live, which it did, for the most part.

John: The first few days were frustrating because recording wasn't the same as playing live. Rothchild held our hands as we learned the process. I didn't know you couldn't have the same "sound" as onstage. "Too live and echo-y," Rothchild said. Paul wanted to damp my drum skins, and it hindered my technique, but after a while I fell in love with the big snare-drum sound it made.

On the second day we laid down the track to "Break On Through." Robby said his guitar melody line was inspired by Butterfield's "Shake Your Money Maker." Jim did a "work" vocal, one that we could hear live in our headphones, but which could be replaced if he wanted. Listening through the phones bothered me so I put one on my right ear and the other on the side of my head so I could hear my drums naturally.

"You should try another vocal, Jim," Paul prodded. "We'll put the new one on another track and you can choose between the two."

Jim nodded and headed back out to the vocal booth.

After stumbling on a second take, Jim did a third, erasing the second because we were out of free tracks. (We were recording on four-track equipment, nothing like today's twenty-four-track recording.)

"I like the first half of the original vocal and the second half of my second performance."

"No problem. Bruce and I will glue them together in the mix."

I found the recording process fascinating—getting a basic rhythm track (drums, bass, and other rhythm instruments), then overdubbing voices and instruments as needed. The danger of so much control was the possibility of losing the feeling, the soul of a song; the advantage was that each of us had the chance to be satisfied with his performance.

Paul Rothchild would soon become known as the "Fifth Door." But, from the beginning, there were others who joined the band in recording sessions. On the first album, session player Larry Knechtel played bass on several songs, while Robby overdubbed bass on "Back Door Man" and "Soul Kitchen," and Ray played his left-handed keyboard bass on "Break On Through."

On the second of its six nights, the recording session reached a climactic high—at least for Rothchild.

Paul: When "The End" was first performed in the studio, we took almost a whole day to set it up, because it was a very complex piece to record. When we finally got the tape rolling, it was the most awe-inspiring thing I'd ever witnessed in a studio. It's still one of the top musical events of my life, and I've made over 160 records.

We were about six minutes into it when I turned to Bruce and said, "Do you understand what's happening here? This is one of the most important moments in recorded rock 'n' roll." Bruce was just a kid then, and said, "Really?" I said, "Stop listening to the sound—it's fine—and listen to the song." When they were done, I had goose bumps from head to foot. It was magic.

Jac: I slipped into the studio during the middle of "The End," becoming totally caught up in that transcendent moment. As the song came to *its* end and the final notes shimmered into silence, the tension in the control room was palpable. God forbid anybody knock over a mike or make a noise. We knew magic when it happened.

Paul: I went into the studio and told them exactly what I just told you and then I asked them to do it again. "Let's make sure we've got it." So they did it again and it was equally brilliant. Afterward, Ray said, "Whew, I don't think we can do that any better." I said, "You don't have to. Between these two takes we have one of the best masters ever cut." It turns out we used the front half of take one and the back half of take two. We did the same thing with "Light My Fire."

My point is, what is on the record is exactly the way The Doors wanted you to hear "The End."

For all the highs at Sunset Sound, and however efficient the sessions —"The total cost was $10,000," Holzman told me, "and it was done in ten days"—there were some early warning signs about Jim Morrison. He and his band may have been making their first record, and they may have been excited—"We were making a record!" Ray exulted— but Jim was too stoned to concern himself with niceties.

"Fuck the mother, kill the father, fuck the mother," Morrison is recalled chanting repeatedly, while Rothchild tried to wait him out. During an early take of "Light My Fire," Manzarek recalled, Morrison noticed that there was a portable TV set on in the room, facing the producer and the engineer, who were in the control room, separated by a large window. The TV was tuned into a Dodgers game. Upset by the distraction, Jim lifted the set and hurled it at the window. (Fortunately, it was tempered glass, and the set bounced back, onto the floor.)

Another night, after a productive evening at the studio, Jim, still buzzing from an LSD high, decided that Sunset Sound was on fire, returned to the studio, grabbed a fire extinguisher and sprayed its contents all over the studio room, soaking down a couple of The Doors' instruments in the process.

The next day, with Elektra having agreed to take care of cleaning up the mess, Jim played innocent child when the other band members quizzed him about the incident. (While scaling a security fence, he'd left a boot behind.)

John: The next day over breakfast at Ah Fong's on Sunset, he pretended not to remember doing it at all. "I did that? Come on, really?"

Ray: We finished recording the album in four more days and left Sunset Sound... still intact and still standing.

In November 1966, The Doors' world changed. With the notoriety they had gained from their stint at the Whisky a Go Go, and with their debut album completed, they were off to New York City for the first time, where they—but mostly Morrison—would be photographed; where they would play the trendy Ondine on the Upper East Side,

*which Manzarek recalls as "the disco of the time—and it was where
Andy Warhol hung out with the Factory denizens."*

*They also continued to pick up random gigs: at a private home in
Montecito; at the tiny Bido Lito's, one of the Hollywood clubs that
had rejected them before, and, best of all, at the Fillmore Auditorium.
Jac Holzman cajoled promoter Bill Graham into booking The Doors
for several weekends, based on his word—and a photograph of
Morrison. On the first weekend, The Doors won over San Francisco.
On the second, the city knocked out The Doors.*

Ray: That first night, we played the Fillmore Auditorium. We get up
on stage and Bill Graham introduces us. "We've got this band from Los
Angeles…" And people are booing Los Angeles.

We come on stage and Jim says, "'When the Music's Over.' Play 'When
the Music's Over.'" I said, "Why are we gonna start with 'When the
Music's Over'? It's a long song, it's slow. We want to just get onstage and
kill them with 'Break On Through.'" Jim said, "No, I've got a feeling, man.
Put everything you can into your playing." OK. Jim had that instinct, so
I started to play and I just put all the power I possibly could into what I
was playing on the organ, and then Densmore comes in with the drums
and they were like cannons, and I thought, I've never had this much
power before! Where did this all come from? It was just brilliant. John
does a *rat-tat-ta-tat-tat* on the drums, and Robby and Jim come in with
a scream and a smashing guitar chord, and it just exploded, and the
audience went "*YEAH!*" And we had them. We had them and they were
ours and we were theirs.

*The following weekend, Morrison managed to miss a show—he later
told Graham that he went to a movie theater and saw* Casablanca
*three times, completely forgetting his engagement. But, Manzarek
says, on Saturday, January 14, 1967, all The Doors went to one of the
biggest shows in town: the opening act to the Summer of Love.*

Ray: We were at our hotel, and somebody said, "Hey, there's a whole
bunch of people going to the park. There's a bunch of bands playing
in the park and everything." And somehow we got out to Golden Gate
Park and there they were, thirty thousand people, Michael McClure
was onstage, Gary Snyder, Allen Ginsberg was playing his harmonium

(below) John adding percussive
comments to Jim's lyrical poetry, 1968

and singing, badly, but he was the most brilliant poetry reader I've ever seen.

It was absolutely amazing. I'd never seen anything like it before. Men in soft garments, women doing that strange dance with their hands twirling around like snakes, almost a primordial kind of goddess-worship dance. It was the beginning of change. What we were going to do was change the whole society, we were going to change the society to be the true America, the real America. We were going to make it a place where we hold these truths to be self-evident, that *all men are created equal.* That was the point of it.

Of course, The Doors are an essential part of the sixties. The sixties were that rare moment of time when the doors of perception for an entire generation opened. The possibilities of the transformation of a society into a more spiritual society actually took place. Hedonistic and at once spiritual, at the same time. The chains and the bounds of repression had been broken and we were free. And the shackles were broken, certainly for black people who could finally get a hamburger in the South sitting next to a white guy. That was over with, that insane segregation of America was over with.

Kids had ingested various hallucinogenic substances—LSD and mushrooms and the rest of it, and opened the doors of perception and found that they were infinite, that they were star children, that they were creatures of energy that belonged in a timeless state of existence, and that state of existence could be called God. For me, growing up a Catholic boy, I looked at my religion and said, "Jesus Christ, it's talking about love! The whole point of it is love, and Jesus was talking about love." Love the Lord, love thy neighbor as thyself. That is exactly what the hippies and the sixties were talking about. Make love, not war. Let's love.

The Fillmore bookings were part of Elektra's promotional campaign for The Doors' debut album. Jac Holzman persuaded promoter Bill Graham to give The Doors two weekends at the rock shrine. And he did more.

Jac: Originally I had promised to release the album in November of 1966 and now I had to talk them out of that. The record was so beautifully realized and important that I wanted to spotlight it free from the crush

of year-end releases. Mid to late January was when albums would start being released again, after everything had been absorbed from Christmas. I wanted to slip it in on the first Monday in January, when there was a wide-open window.

Initially they were disappointed, so I made a commitment that I would release no other album in January. We would focus on The Doors exclusively for that month.

I also promised to take a large, illuminated billboard on the Sunset Strip. This was a new idea for the record business. No one in music had tried it before, but it was my way of saying to everyone in the music community of Los Angeles that Elektra had arrived, and we were big-time serious about a band that had a tenacious local following. It was a message to radio and our distributors that we were willing to spend to make it happen.

TWENTIETH CENTURY FOXES

She's a twentieth century fox
She's a twentieth century fox
No tears, no fears
No ruined years
No clocks
She's a twentieth century fox …

Jim Morrison wrote that one for the love of his life, Pamela Susan Courson. Or did he? As with so much about Morrison, it's not clear. He was not exactly the monogamous type.

Ray: We all assumed that Pam was his main squeeze. Pam was there from the London Fog. There were side girls, peripheral players, Ronnie Harran, the girl who booked the Whisky a Go Go. Billie Winters, who got us into Ondine. Joan Wilson, who was Billy James's secretary. The black girl who was dressed as a Playboy bunny on Halloween night, 1966, at Ondine, the night before we opened there. There were always girls along the line but none of them was like Pamela. I always thought she was his cosmic mate. They were destined for each other.

Morrison, by all accounts, was not a kiss-and-teller, so there were others, including several writers. Eve Babitz says that she met him

(left) "Larger Than Life" – The Doors on their first rock 'n' roll billboard, near the corner of Sunset and Crescent Heights, Los Angeles, 1966

(top) Smiling Pam, backstage at the Whisky, 1966

(bottom) Lynn Krieger getting out of Robby's new Porsche, Los Angeles, 1967

at the London Fog and came onto him before he even sang a note. "Take me home," she said when she was introduced to him. "You're not really going to stay here playing, are you?"

"We don't play," Jim responded. "We work." (Eve's sister, Mirandi, was a clothes designer and a platonic friend of Jim's who made some of his leather outfits.)

Others who hooked up with him ranged from Gloria Stavers, the editor of 16 magazine who famously photographed the band at her New York apartment in 1966, but focused on the lead singer, to Patricia Kennealy, a music journalist who interviewed and says she married Morrison in a witchy ceremony in 1970. Between them came others, from the famous—like Nico, the German model Andy Warhol turned into a "chanteuse" and willed into the Velvet Underground—to the wannabes—young women who kissed and wrote articles and books of wildly varying levels of credibility. Invariably, they claimed to have been the subject of songs Morrison wrote: "Wild Child," "We Could Be So Good Together," and, of course, "L.A. Woman."

Robby: I would never be surprised to hear about Jim getting any female—or male, for that matter! Any female, you know, in Hollywood or otherwise. I was very much in awe—and glad to get the leftovers.

John: I was a little jealous of all the female attention, but I quickly saw that the bright spotlight on the lead singer was dangerous in a way. I was on the edge, so I got … a little singed.

Although both Manzarek and Densmore—along with Pamela's mother, Penny—believe Jim met Pam at the London Fog in spring of 1966, Densmore has admitted that he made a move on her there, only to lose out to Morrison. Close friends of hers say they met at a party some six months before, either at UCLA or at Los Angeles City College, where the eighteen-year-old Pam had been an art student. Born in Weed, California, just south of the Oregon border and a few miles north of Mount Shasta, which Native Americans consider to be a holy mountain. Like Jim, she was in a military family. Her father, Columbus "Corky" Courson, who was a high school principal in nearby Orange County, was also a commander and pilot in the U.S. Navy.

(below) "If I Can Make It There, I Can Make It Anywhere." – Playing before a sold-out crowd in New York City, 1968

Also, like Jim, she was known to be a little wild, an enthusiastic explorer of drugs and of the opposite sex. Her male friends included Tom Baker, a handsome actor who would become a buddy of Morrison's, and Jean de Breteuil, a young French count who'd gone to UCLA and had a reputation as a playboy and drug dealer.

And, like Jim, Pamela was beautiful, almost ethereally so. Like a Michelle Phillips or a Peggy Lipton, she evoked the most romantic notion of the California Girl. "She looked like she stepped out of a page in Vogue magazine," says Penny Courson. Even those who admit her beauty. "She had freckles and red hair and the greenest eyes and just the country-girl glow."

At LACC, she hung out with Mirandi Babitz, who was wise to the ways of the Hollywood scene and happy to take the girl from Orange County under her wing.

Mirandi Babitz: We were doing nothing, you know, wandering around trying to figure out what to do in life. Pam and I were both taking art classes. We were the two obviously hippie girls in this class. I had long straight brown hair with bangs and she had long straight red hair with bangs—and we were both incredibly anorexic and little; I think we weighed about 180 pounds between us. She was real cute, you know, a darling little thing. So we started sitting together…and we became friends."

Outwardly shy, Pamela was stronger than she looked. And, Eve Babitz says, she was fearless. If he said, "Let's drive over this cliff," she said, Pam was the kind of person who actually would. Courson was also known to enjoy partying. She was said to have done some work as a "party girl" and a go-go dancer before Morrison put a stop to it. He had done the same thing with a high school girlfriend, Mary Werbelow, who followed him to Los Angeles with the intention of working on Sunset Strip.

John: Pam had the fire to be Jim's match. Jim liked to dominate women or treat them with great respect. Pam came up to Hollywood to find herself. Instead, she found Jim.

"They just really fell in love at first sight," says Penny Courson, Pamela's mother, who believes they first met at the London Fog. At the

(left) Jim and Pam at the Ambassador Hotel's Coconut Grove, which had temporarily changed its name to the hipper "New Grove," Los Angeles, 1968

(below) Ray and Dorothy at LAX, 1968

club, she says, "Jim had a little bag packed, by the side of the stage." She laughed at the memory. "He was waiting and hoping she'd come back. And one night, she came back, and that was the beginning of the love story. She had a little apartment, and he went home with her."

Paul Rothchild: With her, at home, he could just be Jim. He could have smelly feet and be a human being and she accepted it.

Not that she would ever accept his bad-boy antics. She could crack a pretty mean whip.

And he'd like that. That was fun for him because very few people were willing to go on the offensive with him. I guess he liked that about her. She just had enough guts to go on the offensive.

Bill Siddons (former manager): Pamela said something to me in Paris that never left me. She said, "There were a lot of people who pretended to be close to Jim, but I was the only one who had the nerve to stand up to him."

All the rest of us just went, "OK, Jim, whatever you want, Jim, we'll work around it." But Pamela didn't. She loved him to death, but she was not willing to be abused. Pamela just went, *"Fuck you, buddy! You'd better do this!"* She didn't take any shit from him. So inevitably he went back to her, because he knew that she was willing to lose him. She had a sense of personal integrity that Jim found irresistible.

And when Pam told her parents that she was dating a young man who was in a rock band, they had no problem with it.

Penny Courson: I had no objection, but it was sort of funny the first time she was going to bring Jim home. Cork and I were having a dinner party. Judith (Pam's older sister) was dating an English professor. Cork's aunt and mother were there, kind of the matriarchs of the family, and I had prepared them for the fact that this young man was a musician and his hair was long, and they arrived, and the guy had short hair. It was Tom Baker! Pam had had a fight with Jim and brought Tom instead. I thought, "Well, I'm not going to say anything." And Grandmother said, "You're a nice young man. You had your hair cut!"

The next time they came home, she brought Jim. He was just the essence of perfection of manners: genteel, wonderful, and he completely charmed us.

I remember we were having cocktails, and Cork asked if he'd like something, and he said a martini on the rocks. I went in the kitchen to make dinner, and he came in and asked—and he was whispering— "Could you add some water to this? It's a little strong!"

Ray Manzarek and his college sweetheart, Dorothy Fujikawa, were living together. At Ondine, the disco The Doors played in late 1966, Robby met Lynn Veres, and began dating her when she moved to Los Angeles. Although she also briefly dated Morrison, it was Krieger who won her over in 1970. ("He was mad," says Krieger. "He admitted he blew one there.") They married in 1972.

(below) Robby: "The fans were going completely wild for us."

(right) Jim caught in the closet with a blond bombshell at the famous Chateau Marmont Hotel, Hollywood, 1968

That left Densmore still playing the field. Of course, so was the lead singer.

Morrison "was Michelangelo's **David**, *physically," said Densmore. Noting that magazines ranging from teenybopper fanzines to* **Vogue** *were featuring photo spreads on Jim, Howard Smith of the* **Village Voice** *wrote: "There really hasn't been a major male sex symbol since James Dean died and Marlon Brando got a paunch. Dylan is more of a cerebral heartthrob and The Beatles have always been too cute to be deeply sexy. Now along comes Jim Morrison of The Doors. If my antennae are right, he could be the biggest thing to grab the mass libido in a very long time. I have never seen such an animalistic response from so many different kinds of women."*

At a time when the mainstream press was resistant to giving space to rock culture, the **New York Times Magazine** *noted that Morrison was being talked about as "the most potent sex symbol to come along in our popular culture since Jimmy Dean and Elvis Presley."*

The magazines weren't the only ones who saw Morrison as a commodity. Elektra had photographer Joel Brodsky shoot The Doors— again, with a focus on the lead singer—and the results included what's become legend as the "young lion" poses of a shirtless Jim wearing only a strand of colored beads he got from Gloria Stavers the night before. Apparently, she shot him, and then she got him.

Bill Siddons: I knew there were other ones—of course you'd have to be blind not to know there were other ones—but I knew ultimately Pamela was always the only real one.

Jim himself indicated as much when, in February 1969, he signed a will leaving his entire estate to Pam. And if she were to die within three months of his own death, his fortune would then be divided between his sister and brother.

(below) Robby with a fan literally hanging on him, New York, 1968

(right) Robby gives a fan a studio tour, Los Angeles, 1968

5 "GIRL, WE COULDN'T GET MUCH HIGHER"

THE DOORS

**BREAK ON THROUGH
WITH AN
ELECTRIFYING ALBUM**

5 "GIRL, WE COULDN'T GET MUCH HIGHER"

The Doors were immediate critics' darlings. In their own hometown, where they'd caused a fuss at the Whisky, only to earn a short, lukewarm notice from the Los Angeles Times, their debut album received a similarly mixed review. Pete Johnson found Morrison "somewhat overmannered, murky, and dull." In "The End," he noted, Morrison exhibited "how bored he can sound as he recites singularly simple, over-elaborated psychedelic non sequiturs and fallacies." Johnson judged "Break On Through," "Twentieth Century Fox," and "Alabama Song" to be "fairly good." So much for the hometown advantage.

In the underground paper, the L.A. Free Press, Gene Youngblood remarked: "The Beatles and The Stones are for blowing your mind, but The Doors are for afterward, when your mind is already gone."

Paul Williams, founder and editor of Crawdaddy!, called the debut "flawless." He wrote: "The Doors is an album of magnitude ... The Doors have been delivered to the public full-grown and still growing ... The birth of a group is in this album and it's as good as anything in rock."

In Hullabaloo magazine, record producer and critic Paul Nelson wrote: "The Doors ... is a record which balances a lot of seeming paradoxes: expert, controlled, and precise in attack, the group nonetheless excels in performances which grow from pregnant understatement to exhilarating incandescence in a matter of seconds.

"The Doors are the new group by which all other new groups must, for a time at least, be measured."

And in the retrospective reflection that time allows, Mikal Gilmore, writing in Rolling Stone in 1991, noted: "The Doors' impact on 1967 was enormous—and singular. Bands such as The Beatles, like many artists from the Bay Area scene, were touting a fusion of music, drugs, and idealism that they hoped would reform and redeem a troubled age—and benign as those intentions may have been, they were still troubling to many observers. By contrast, The Doors were fashioning music that looked at prospects of hedonism and violence, of revolt and chaos, and embraced those prospects unflinchingly."

Despite their best efforts, The Doors' first single, "Break On Through," didn't. And the guys did more than pose for photos and do press interviews. They went to Elektra's offices and got on the phones.

Ray: All four of us were dialing the radio stations. And you'd raise the pitch of your voice a little. "Hi, I wanna hear that boss song from The Doors! They're our L.A. band! Play that "Break On Through." And eventually the girl or the deejay or whoever was taking the calls would say, "All right, just stop calling. We know you're with the band or they're paying you to do it, so just stop."

As it turned out, their first major hit was only a razor blade cut away. By early 1967, a number of underground stations had cropped up in New York, San Francisco, Los Angeles, and other major cities, taking over undervalued FM signals. The stations featured disc jockeys with countercultural

SOLEMNLY PUBLISH AND DECLARE, THAT
THESE COLONIES ARE AND OF RIGHT
OUGHT TO BE FREE AND INDEPENDENT
STATES ... AND FOR THE SUPPORT OF THIS
DECLARATION, WITH A FIRM RELIANCE
ON THE PROTECTION OF DIVINE
PROVIDENCE, WE MUTUALLY PLEDGE
OUR LIVES, OUR FORTUNES AND OUR
SACRED HONOUR.

tendencies—many of them were escapees from formatted AM radio—and they gave birth to "free-form radio," playing whatever they wanted, whenever they wanted. For them, lengthy songs like "Light My Fire" were no problem, and the song gained extensive airplay.

But that was underground FM. Elektra needed a shorter version for Top 40 stations, and Jac Holzman asked The Doors to try to cut one. When that failed, Rothchild returned to the studio—without the guys in the band.

Ray: We got a call, saying "We've got it. Come on down." I thought they'd tighten the solos…We listened to it, and there are no edits through the second verse and chorus, and here comes Ray's solo—and it's gone. And so is Robby's. We looked at each other and said, "Wait a minute, you've cut out all the solos. You've gone from the start of the organ solo right to the very end of the solos, back to the beginning introduction riff. Holy cow!" We said, "It's horrible. You cut the heart of the song." But Paul said, "Remember, you're a kid in Minnesota. You've never heard the song before. Now what do you think of it?" And my god, it works. It's verse/chorus, verse/chorus, short, eight-bar solo, repeat the introduction, verse/chorus, verse/chorus, and out. And Robby says, "I hate it. But I love it."

While Elektra rolled out "Light My Fire" as a single, The Doors began looking for someone to take care of business. Up to now, they'd relied on Robby's father for advice, and on attorney Max Fink for legal help. They needed management, and someone to book their gigs.

Robby: We had to try hard in those days just to get a gig, and then we'd have to try hard to get Jim there on time. So we said, why should we do this? We ought to get a manager to babysit."

They found Asher Dann and Sal Bonafede. Dann was a Realtor to the stars who loved to hang out and wanted in on the entertainment industry. To do so, he teamed with Bonafede, whose management resume included the doo-wop Top 40 group Dion and the Belmonts. The two men introduced The Doors to a booking agency and a publicity firm; their concert prices suddenly increased, and led by their first hit

In June, "Light My Fire" accomplished what the first single did not: It broke into Billboard magazine's Hot 100. By early July, it had made it into the Top 20. Two weeks later, it was in the Top Ten. The top spot was occupied by The Association with "Windy," but "Light My Fire" reached No. 3 for the week ending July 22, 1967. And then, the next week, it happened. The Doors were No. 1 in the country and, for three weeks, "Light My Fire" would remain at the top of the charts.

Ray: It was virtually two years to the week, in the middle or the third week in July, when Jim sang "Moonlight Drive" to me on the beach. Two years later we had the number one song in America, and it was like "Holy shit! Fucking amazing! This is the plan! This *was* the plan."

Now here's the fun of what we did: We were envisioning a plan, a scheme, something to happen in the future and we were going to implement all of our ideas and put them into reality, dreaming of having a rock 'n' roll band, making it to the top, and doing all the things that you have to do to make it to the top. It was absolutely amazing. I think the most pleasurable thing for my ego and probably for Jim's is that we preconceived this happening and then it happened, and it's like *"Yeahhh!"* And once that happens, you know that anything is possible. At that point I thought, "Let's make more dreams. Let's keep on playing rock 'n' roll, of course. But then let's make some films. And then politics!"

But first, said Elektra, let's make another album, and let's keep promoting The Doors. And so it was that they were booked for **The Ed Sullivan Show** for September 17. Although this mainstream variety show on CBS was as square as its host's hunched shoulders, it was mandatory viewing on Sunday nights for rock music fans. Here was where Elvis made his first, biggest splash, in 1956. In Los Angeles, a ten-year-old Robby Krieger was watching, and found his first idol. "It was just, it was amazing, it was like this guy was just so cool, man, nobody I'd ever seen was that cool. Everybody wanted to be like him, you know. Even James Dean, obviously."

As soon as he could, Robby dashed out to the record shop. "We bought an EP that had "Don't Be Cruel," "Hound Dog," "I want you, I need you, I love you," which I later recorded, and "Mystery Train."

5 "GIRL, WE COULDN'T GET MUCH HIGHER"

(below) Jim "walking the edge" during a
surprise encore, Copenhagen, 1968

And now, after Elvis, after The Beatles, and after The Rolling Stones, it was The Doors' turn.

Ray: It was funny. Dorothy and I were watching *The Ed Sullivan Show* to see the rock act that was on, and at the end of the show, he said, "And next week, coming up, the boys with that 'Light My Fire,' The Doors from Los Angeles will be playing." And we looked at each other and said, "Holy shit, we're on *The Ed Sullivan Show* next week." We didn't know anything about it until our TV told us. I called John and Robby, and they had seen it too.

And man, we were proud. This was like, "We're on the fuckin' *Ed Sullivan Show!*" But when you get there to do it, it was another TV show gig, running around, there're cameras, "OK, get the boys, Doors, you're on, it's a rehearsal, play the song."

But it wasn't quite that simple. As Manzarek noted in his book: "Paul and Bruce flew out from L.A. to handle the sound for us. After all, The Ed Sullivan Show was live and we weren't about to turn the mixing of our sound over to some old TV union guys … we wanted everything to be right. This was the real deal. This was Ed Sullivan. A national institution."

After the sound check, while The Doors were in the dressing room, Sullivan himself popped in. He'd seen the rehearsal and had a bit of advice. "You know, you boys are really handsome. But you'd look a lot better if you'd smile more."

To which Morrison responded: "We're kind of a sullen group."

The band's next visitor was the show's producer, who told them that CBS would have a problem with a line from "Light My Fire:" "Girl we couldn't get much higher." "Higher," he said, could not be uttered on national television.

Morrison and Manzarek agreed to come up with another word. When the producer left, they told Krieger and Densmore that they'd do the song as it was. And they did. Morrison did not, as he was depicted in the movie, emphasize "higher." But he did sing it.

Ray: And with Botnick and Rothchild doing the sound, no one could hit the delay button when we actually said the word "higher." That was the irony of it.

After the show, the producer was livid. "Mr. Sullivan wanted you for six more shows. Well, you'll never work The Ed Sullivan Show again!"

Ray: So Jim said, "Hey, man, we just did *The Ed Sullivan Show*." And then he said, after that great Normal Mailer line, "Once a philosopher, twice a pervert." The guy went, *"Ehhh,"* heard the word "pervert," and stormed out. It didn't matter to us. We got the No. 1 song in America; what the hell is another appearance on *The Ed Sullivan Show* going to do for us? I don't think anybody was concerned. So what? We blew it. We said "higher" on national television.

One more thing. The band looked sullen.

Densmore and Krieger do fess up to the fact that they let family members know that they would be on the iconic TV show. As for Morrison, who'd cut his family ties, he let his band's success catch his parents and siblings by surprise.

In 1965 and 1966, while Jim and the other Doors were getting together, working the clubs, and signing with Elektra Records, the Morrison family was in London, where the admiral was stationed.

Andy: The next thing I knew, we went back in '67. I graduated from high school in Arlington, Virginia, and that summer, my friend Mike Winters from Coronado called up and said, "We got this album of The Doors and it's got your brother's name." And having known Jim from having met him, summer vacation and Easter or Christmas, Mike said, "It looks like your brother." Well, I'd been listening to "Light My Fire" on the radio for a couple of months, and I went down and got the album, brought it home and showed my mother, and there was Jim.

Andy has been quoted describing an uneasy scene when his parents heard the album. In the seminal Morrison biography, No One Here Gets Out Alive, Andy said that his father was reading his newspaper and that, at the end of "The End," his paper began to shake violently.

5 "GIRL, WE COULDN'T GET MUCH HIGHER"

(below) Filming *The Doors Are Open* at
the Roundhouse, London, 1968

Andy: My mother listened to it; I don't think my dad ever listened to the whole album. And none of us ever took "The End" very seriously. We took it as the Oedipus Rex syndrome. We never took it about being personal about our home and family life.

If, in fact, Jim's parents were upset by their son, Clara Morrison wouldn't have sent a copy of that first album to her daughter, who stayed in London through 1968.

Anne: I had no idea what he was doing. My mom was back in the States and she sent me an album. I was astounded that that was my brother on the cover. Then I started to hear it all around town.

The music scene was big there and I fell in love with the music right away and started hearing it. I'd even stop at doors and be amazed that other people were listening to it. Everyone was listening to it.

Andy: I called The Doors' office and found out he was playing at the Scene in New York, and I just went up there and they told me what hotel he was staying at, and I just knocked on the door and he looked at me and says, "Huh, you're my brother, aren't you?" So then he let me hang out.

STRANGE DAYS

Even before "Light My Fire" became a hit, The Doors began work on their next album, which would be called Strange Days. With Morrison and Krieger having built up a stockpile of songs, they had several left over from their first album. But one of their strongest compositions was a new one, the result of a long, strange night that Krieger and Densmore found themselves forced to spend with Morrison.

Robby: Jim showed up at the house in Laurel Canyon where John and I lived. He was very depressed and he was talking about killing himself, which wasn't that unusual, but we believed him, like we usually did. "He just didn't think it was worth it anymore, and life was horrible. John was there, and Georgie Newton, a girlfriend of ours. And so we spent all night talking him out of killing himself, and in the morning we said, "OK, Jim, maybe if we go up to the top of the hill and watch the sun come up, maybe that will do something for you." So we went up to the top of

Laurel Canyon, and we watched the sun come up. Lo and behold, Jim's mood changed all of a sudden, and he came up with the song "People Are Strange," and said, "Man, I've just seen the light. It was so beautiful up there, I wrote a song on the way back down the hill." Up there, he realized that, "Hey, when you're strange, things are gonna be messed up, but if, from within, you see the sun come up and everything's cool, then it's all you; it's a projection of yourself."

He wrote that down and then I came up with the music about an hour later. We recorded it the next day.

Ray: *Strange Days* is when we began to experiment with the studio itself, as an instrument to be played. It was now eight-track, and we thought, "My goodness, we can do all kinds of things. The first album was four-track, but now we've got eight tracks to play with." It seems like nothing in these days of digital recording, but to us, those eight tracks were really liberating. So, at that point, we began to play—it became five people: keyboards, drums, guitar, singer, and studio."

Well, there were also Paul Rothchild and Bruce Botnick again. And another session bassist, Doug Lubahn, from the band Clearlight.

With the team assembled, The Doors recorded several of the songs that didn't make it into the debut album, including "Moonlight Drive"—which, Manzarek notes, got funkier, and evolved into a "rock tango"—"My Eyes Have Seen You," which was the second song Morrison sang to Manzarek on the beach in Venice, and the electrifying "When the Music's Over," which many read as The Doors' first political anthem, with Morrison's fevered cry, "We want the world and we want it … NOW!!!!"

The bouncy "Love Me Two Times" was the second song Robby Krieger came up with after Morrison's homework assignment during rehearsals. The song was inspired, he said, by the idea of lovers being separated, and, particularly, in the case of a young man going off to war. Whatever its message, when it was released as a single, many radio stations refused to play it, deeming it too risqué.

There was "Horse Latitudes," built on the poem Jim wrote in high school. There was "Unhappy Girl," for which Rothchild, enjoying the tech toys of the day, and inspired by The Beatles' new album Sgt. Pepper's Lonely Hearts Club Band, *suggested that Manzarek play his keyboard part backward. (And he did.)*

And there was "You're Lost Little Girl," a Krieger song for which The Doors had high hopes. "We wanted Frank Sinatra to cover it," said Manzarek. "It was just at the time that he was breaking up with Mia Farrow, and we could hear Frank singing it to her."

Ray: *Strange Days* was a commentary on the times. But it was a commentary on post–World War II America more than just the sixties. The Doors were not so much commenting on the hippie era. Our perspective was broader than just the here and now. We had a beatnik foundation, a literary foundation, a film foundation."

In June, when, by all rights, The Doors should have been a featured attraction at the Monterey Pop Festival in California, the band was on an East Coast tour of nightclubs and small theaters. Theories vary on why The Doors weren't in Monterey, along with such peers as The Byrds, The Who, The Mamas & the Papas, Jimi Hendrix, Big Brother & the Holding Company (whose lead singer, Janis Joplin, gave a breakout performance), Jefferson Airplane, and Simon & Garfunkel.

Morrison himself thought it was because The Doors were perceived as an L.A. band, and Monterey was just south of San Francisco. But the three-day outdoor festival featured bands from around the world, including several from Los Angeles.

Well, then, it was because Lou Adler was one of the organizers, and he remembered Morrison's smart-ass comeback when he'd rejected the band's demo.

There was also the tour, which had The Doors playing the Action House, a dance club out on Long Island. The Doors had just played a few nights at Steve Paul's Scene in Manhattan and knew that the club

5 "GIRL, WE COULDN'T GET MUCH HIGHER"

(below) In the Victorian Greenhouse, San
Francisco, 1968

was shutting down during the Monterey Pop weekend. When he tried
to connect with Nico, he learned that she, too, was in Monterey—and
with Brian Jones of The Rolling Stones. At the Action House, he put
away one straight bourbon after another until showtime. Onstage, he
tried to take his clothes off and had to be led offstage by road manager
Bill Siddons.

After the show, Densmore declared his disgust with Morrison. But,
although he threatened to leave, he never did for long.

In the eyes of the other Doors, Densmore was uptight. Maybe he
was, Densmore said, but, he added, "I psychically knew Jim was on
a dark path, and it disturbed me. As his self-destruction increased,
Ray and Robby trying to ignore it disturbed me even more than Jim
going down."

Krieger and Manzarek were more benign, with Ray noting that, for all
his faults, Morrison missed only a couple of concerts in The Doors'
five years of performing. Krieger, however, couldn't help relating the
Ice Cream Incident.

Robby: The only time we blew a show was at the University of Michigan
when Jim got really too drunk, and the reason for that was ice cream. Let
me explain: We were driving to the show, and John and I and Ray said,
"Hey, there's a homemade ice cream place. Let's stop there." Jim said,
"No, come on, I hate ice cream." He had an aversion to certain foods,
and he had a worse aversion to watching people eat certain foods. It
just drove him nuts. But we did it anyway. We stopped and had the ice
cream. He was smoldering in the backseat. So he starts drinking. By the
time we got onstage, he was just so out of it that all he could do was try
to do a couple of blues or something, and John just couldn't stand it; he
left the stage, and pretty soon I left, and these poor people—Ray tried
to go on for a little while, but we blew the whole thing.

A week after their September appearance on **The Ed Sullivan Show**,
Strange Days came out. Once again, The Doors earned critical
raves. Now, it was time to get out and promote it. The band played
a diverse mix of college gigs, clubs, and Bill Graham venues,
including, in one November weekend, both the Fillmore Auditorium
and the Winterland Arena in San Francisco.

On the twenty-fifth, The Doors have a concert in Washington, D.C. That's close to where his parents are living. Clara Morrison sets off, with Andy in tow, to try to see her Jimmy.

Andy: My mother got tickets and took my girlfriend and me. It was at the Washington Hilton. My mother hadn't seen him since '65 and she was trying to get backstage; she's telling the guys who she is and they said, "As soon as he gets off, we'll set up a meeting. Go wait in the waiting room." Well, they left her sitting there and he ducked out, and I remember my mother was driving my girlfriend and I home and she was crying and I felt bad for her.

Why do you think Jim did that?

Andy: He didn't want a big emotional display in front of his friends. He didn't dislike my parents. He told me that you can't do it halfway with the family thing. He said, "Maybe later on we'll get back together. I can't come home for Christmas dinner one time and then take off and do my thing because they're going to want to see me again and again and again. You can't be a part-time son. They're going to want all or nothing." He said it's easier for him at that time, being young, doing his own thing and getting in trouble in the media, just to separate.

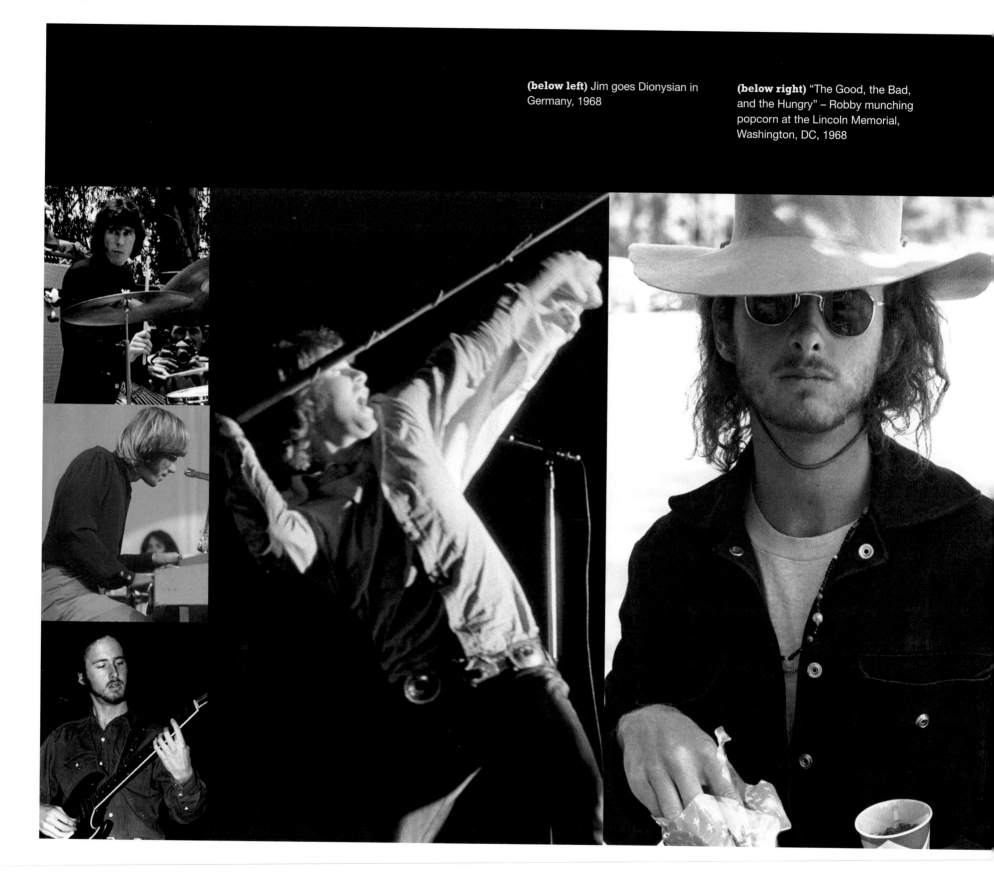

(below left) Jim goes Dionysian in Germany, 1968

(below right) "The Good, the Bad, and the Hungry" – Robby munching popcorn at the Lincoln Memorial, Washington, DC, 1968

6 CHAOS: THE ROAD TO FREEDOM

6 CHAOS: THE ROAD TO FREEDOM

Jim (*in his Elektra Records bio*): I've always been attracted to ideas that were about revolt against authority—when you make your peace with authority you become an authority. I like ideas about the breaking away or overthrowing of established order—I am interested in anything about revolt, disorder, chaos, especially activity that seems to have no meaning. It seems to me to be the road to freedom.

Paul Ferrara and Frank Lisciandro, friends from the UCLA film school days, were two of several buddies of Jim's and Ray's who began shooting a documentary in the summer of 1967. Funded by The Doors and called Feast of Friends, *the film covered the band on the road, where Morrison appeared to be acting up for the cameras, doing his best to incite fans—and cops—at various concerts.*

Too many people, Lisciandro thinks, took his "chaos" remark "to mean he was an anarchist, a revolutionary, or, worse, a nihilist. Hardly anyone noticed that Jim was restating Rimbaud and the Surreal poets, artists and thinkers like Andre Breton, Marcel Duchamp, Luis Bunuel, and Louis Aragon."

Frank: Almost all of his friends, and most of the journalists who chronicled his actions, saw Jim's lifestyle as self-destructive. But looking at it in the light of the ancient oracle/poet tradition, his lifestyle could be called self-*instructive:* a way of learning about the nature of things by risking the derangement of the senses. It was his occupation and vocation. He did it the way he did everything, without reservation and to the extreme limit of his abilities.

Many writers did dwell on Jim Morrison's erratic behavior—his daredevil, death-taunting stunts, like jumping out of a moving car or walking on a fifteenth story ledge over Sunset Boulevard, like threatening a girlfriend with a knife and hosing down a studio within hours of his first professional recording session.

But all he was doing was signaling and reflecting who he was, from childhood to twentysomething; from personal life to onstage persona. Just as he would collapse in a school corridor, or lay still on the ground, feigning death, so now he would drop, faux dead, onstage. He attacked his microphone and other equipment, puzzled the band with his sudden silences, surprised them with improvised interjections of his poetry, teased and abused the audiences, and drove cops and security guards mad enough to cuff him, arrest him, and beat him up.

He could never be a straight-ahead performer, an entertainer, any more than he could be a normal human being.

Jim: The only time I really open up is onstage. I feel spiritual up there. Performing gives me a mask, a place to hide myself where I can reveal myself. I see it as more than performing, going on, doing songs, and leaving. I take everything personally, and don't really feel I've done a complete job unless we've gotten everybody in the theater on common ground.

In his first article for Rolling Stone, *in early 1968, Jerry Hopkins, who would become the fledgling rock newspaper's Los Angeles correspondent, told about seeing The Doors at the Shrine Auditorium and,*

(previous spread) Jim enraptured by the muse during the recording of *Strange Days*, 1967

(below) Jim in the throes of "Light My Fire" at the Roundhouse, London, 1968.

(left) Jim watches as Ray breaks into a solo and John flails away at the drums at the legendary Hollywood Bowl, Los Angeles, 1968.

as a fan of long standing, coming away somewhat disappointed. At nightclubs, he simply stood, often hanging onto the microphone for dear life, and sang. Now, he was moving around much more, and, on occasion, dropping suddenly, "as if he'd been shotgunned...or kicked in the scrotum."

Hopkins was pleased, he said, that "one piece of stage business missing at the Shrine performance was Morrison's carefully executed "accidental" fall from the stage into the crowd."

(This followed what Ray Manzarek called the "tightrope walk," perfected at a huge dance club called The Cheetah, where Jim pranced along the very edge of a very high stage.) "For months," Hopkins wrote, "this had been a part of the act. It got a lot of screams from the teenyboppers. Then a review appeared in a local newspaper that called the fall one of the phoniest things ever."

Pamela DesBarres, the groupie who had a playful and druggy—but platonic—friendship with Morrison, remembered seeing Morrison doing what's now known as a stage dive as far back as May of 1967. They had returned to the Whisky for the first time since being banished, forever, the previous August. (What a difference an album makes.)

Pamela DesBarres: It was a swan dive, the kind I was trying to do at the YWCA in the summer of '56, only Jim Morrison didn't hold his nose. He just let go of himself and careened into the black hole, knowing the masses would hold him up. He came to us, like no one had done before, and no one would do again.

Penny Courson: He invented the mosh pit!

Jim: I just think I'm lucky. I've found a perfect medium to express myself in. Music, writing, theatre, action—I'm doing all those things. I like to write...I find that music liberates my imagination. When I sing my songs in public, that's a dramatic act, but not just acting as in theatre, but as social act, real action.

But there were several forces at work, beyond Jim's love of shock and chaos. There was the growing size of The Doors' audience and, therefore, the size of the venues they played. There were changing

the expectations and demands of their audience, shifting from college students digging the darkness to teenaged girls digging on the leather-clad "Lizard King." There was his own evolving love of the stage and interest in theatrics. And there were the drugs and the alcohol that fueled it all.

Jim: I was less theatrical, less artificial when I began, but now the audiences we play for are much larger and the rooms wider. It's necessary to project more. I think when you're a small dot at the end of a large arena, you have to make up for that lack of intimacy with expanded movements."

Bill Siddons: Jim was kind of being worshipped into a box, and he was really victimized by it. "OK you're the crazy Jim Morrison! You've got to jump off the stage and reappear in a cloud of smoke!"

Jim: In a large concert situation, I think histrionics are necessary because it gets to be more than just a musical event. It turns into a bit of a spectacle. I'm too conscious of what's happening. I don't like to be too objective about it. I like to just let it happen—direct it a little consciously, maybe, but just kind of follow the vibrations I get in each particular circumstance. We don't plan theatrics.

Robby: Morrison was one of the few if not the only performer I knew who really believed what he was saying. He lived that life. He wasn't just up there doing his trip and then he'd go home and watch TV and have a beer and laugh at it all, laugh all the way to the bank. He was a guy that, he lived that life that he lived out onstage all the time. And when he went home, it was just some cheap motel somewhere, and he just hung out until the next show, you know. Sometimes he would be the greatest guy you'd ever want to meet—super polite, together, clean, and everything else—but the next day, he'd be completely the other way. All those stories are true, most of them: He lived his whole life right on the edge, and people could sense that when he was onstage; there was always something under there, ready to happen—and if they were lucky that night, it might happen. All I can say is that he was totally committed to living the life of the revolution.

Ray: That's why we got jumped on, I guess. We were revolutionaries. A revolutionary rock 'n' roll band. And the only message The Doors ever

preached was freedom. That's the joke of it all. Just freedom. Individual human rights.

John: It was a religious experience between us and the audience. Sometimes those early days at the Fillmore in New York, *phew,* it was just scary at times. Maybe Jim would get hurt or something—not from the audience attacking us or anything, just that it got so heavy you just wondered if something weird was going to happen, 'cause Jim was so intense. Like I said, it was religious. It was just—this sounds really *"We were all together,"* but we *were* together, the audience and us. They just went crazy. Everybody went, "Yeah!" And that was it. It was just incredible.

Jim: Maybe you could call us erotic politicians. We're a rock 'n' roll band, a blues band, just a band, but that's not all. A Doors concert is a public meeting called by us for a special kind of dramatic discussion and entertainment. When we perform, we're participating in the creation of a world, and we celebrate that with the audience. It becomes the sculpture of bodies in action. That's politics, but our power is sexual. We make concerts sexual politics. The sex starts with me, then moves out into the charmed circle of musicians onstage, then the music we make goes out to include the audience and interacts with them: They go home and interact with the rest of reality, then I get it all back by interacting with that reality … so the whole sex thing works out to be one big ball of fire …

If Morrison sounded a little too polished and practiced with his soundbites … well, maybe he was. Not long before, he'd been interviewed before a concert in Cleveland. Asked to define his act, he responded: "Easy, man. It's not an act. It's politics. We're erotic politicians."

Q: What are your interests?
Jim: Anything that has to do with revolt, disorder, chaos, activity that's got no meaning.
Q: What has meaning?
Jim: Things that seem to have no meaning.

Jim: Music is very erotic. One of the functions is a purgation of emotion. To call our music orgasmic means that we are able to move people to a kind of emotional orgasm through the medium of words and music.

A concert clicks when the musicians and the audience reach a kind of united experience. It is stirring and satisfying to know that the various boundaries which separate people from other people are lowered for the space of one hour.

Robby: One point that we haven't discussed is the aspect of terror that he would instill sometimes. I think it's an important part of his personality, which I think the audience would feel sometimes. Sometimes he would just take it to the edge.

John Densmore: And he'd stick the microphone down into somebody's mouth. "Come on, what do you have to say about yourself?" So it got kind of rowdy. And there was a lot of this *"Uh, uh, uh."* And he would wait. There'd be long silences where we'd be riffing and I'd run out of fills, and he'd wait longer. But he'd do it just to get the audience to squirm a little, and then maybe say something.

NEW HAVEN: "SAY YOUR THING, MAN!"

In December 1967, The Doors had a gig in New Haven, Connecticut. This was a fund-raiser for New Haven College's Interfraternity Scholarship Fund. At the New Haven Arena, while the audience gathered, Morrison was whiling away some time.

Jim: There were all these little rooms backstage, see, and I was talking to a girl in one of the rooms—it was actually a shower room, I guess. Then this cop came in and started hassling me and sprayed some gas in my eyes—it blinds you temporarily—and finally someone told him that I was with The Doors and was supposed to be there, or something like that. The cop let me go. Later, when I was onstage, I was singing "Back Door Man" and in the middle I started telling the crowd what had happened backstage.

In his book, **Riders on the Storm,** *John Densmore tells the story from his perspective, atop the drum riser. Just before going onstage, road manager Vince Treanor had moved the drums.*

John: He told me that Jim had been maced in one of the dressing rooms by a policeman.

(below) Jim coming offstage in Vancouver as "the man" watches closely.

…When Jim came onstage, I could sense that something confrontational was going to happen. His eyes were red and he looked mad. In the middle of "Back Door Man," Jim told the story of the backstage incident.

Jim: I want to tell you about something that happened just two minutes ago right here in New Haven…This is New Haven, Connecticut, United States of America!

… We started talking
And we wanted some privacy
So we went into the shower room
We were not doing anything, you know,
Just standing there and talking.

Morrison was talk-singing his story over the song's instrumental break, and the band, which had grown accustomed to rolling with whatever punches their vocalist might throw, laid down a musical bed for him, accenting the story, just as Morrison did, imitating a redneck drawl…

And this little man came up,
This little man,
In a little blue suit and a little blue cap,
And said, "Whatcha doin' there?"
"Nothin'."
But he did not go away
He stood there and then
He reached around behind him
And he brought out this little can of somethin'
Looked like shaving cream
And then he sprayed it into my eyes.
I was blinded for about thirty minutes!

Manzarek, hunched over his organ as always, remembered Morrison telling the audience: "I thought their motto was 'protect and serve.' The fascists!"

The Doors may not have known that things were tense in the town of New Haven. The police had been accused of using too much force at an antiwar rally just days before. Now, here were several officers stationed in front of the stage, facing the audience. As Morrison rapped, they began to turn around and glare at him. Not only was he taunting them, he was revving up the crowd. According to Michael Zwerin, a rock journalist who wrote about the concert for Cheetah *magazine, several girls near the stage began calling the police "pigs."*

As Morrison finally returned to singing "Back Door Man," the house lights came on. Morrison demanded that the lights be dimmed, but a police officer known as Lieutenant Kelly walked onstage and informed Morrison that the show was over, and that he was under arrest. As another cop joined Lt. Kelly, Morrison offered his microphone to Kelly. "Say your thing, man." Instead, the cops did their thing, hauling an incredulous Morrison off the stage and down the back stairs.

Backstage, Morrison was witnessed being pummeled and kicked by two other cops, who then took him to jail, charging him with obscenity and resisting arrest. Later, police also arrested Zwerwin and a reporter and photographer from Life *magazine. The photographer, Tim Page, had recently returned from an assignment in Vietnam, and caught the police beating a young man.*

The charges against the journalists—and Morrison—were ultimately dropped. But Life *would run a spread on the concert, and the* New York Times *published a story, noting that it was the first time a rock musician had been arrested onstage.*

The Doors had won a skirmish against the police, but the incident did cost the band some business. Concert promoters began to cast a wary eye on the band, and, according to Robby Krieger, radio stations and record retailers began pulling the band's new album, Strange Days, *and its first single, "People Are Strange" off the shelves and off the air. The album, which critics recognized as an excellent follow-up to* The Doors' *debut effort, went gold, but neither "People Are Strange" nor "Love Me Two Times" cracked the Top Ten.*

Something else happened in the aftermath of New Haven. The audience changed. Sure, the young girls were still fixated on Jim Morrison. But now, rock fans began to go to Doors concerts expecting something more than favored artists doing familiar songs. They were looking, in a way, to see something go wrong.

Ray: After the New Haven bust, the vice squad would come…People would come to see this sex god, and to see what he was up to."

To Manzarek, Morrison was nothing less than a rock shaman.

Ray: The shaman was the seer of the tribe. He would go into trances, and the people would have special days—feast days and ceremonies—where they would sit around and play on drums and rattles and play rhythms, and the shaman would stand in the middle of this circle of people and go into a trance, and his spirit would leave his body and go on these psychedelic journeys in which he would see what might be wrong with somebody in the tribe; what the weather is going to be like next year; what the harvest is going to be; what kind of psychic crisis this tribe might be going through. He was a spiritual guide, and Jim Morrison was that same kind of guide onstage.

A Doors concert became a shamanistic rite. I tripped out all the time; I'd be playing and trip myself out on what I was playing, and Jim would be gone in the first five minutes; John and Robby and I would start the rhythms going and five minutes after we'd start, Jim would be gone, man, he would be off, and we'd be following him. Sometimes we'd lead him, other times he'd lead us, and the audience would follow the four of us. And we'd go on these little voyages into the dark side of the soul and into the light and into the weird side—into sex, into violence, into the boogeyman, into God—and it would just be journeys swimming, swimming through the void.

JIM THE DRUNK

But, for all of Manzarek's theories about Morrison the Dionysian, or Morrison the shaman, The Doors also had to deal with Morrison the alcoholic.

Jerry Hopkins and Danny Sugerman, in their book, ran through a partial drink list: "Gin stingers one day, whiskey with beer chasers the next, Black Russians on the third, tequila neat the fourth, Singaore Slings or some other tropical drink with fruit when he was hungry."

When I interviewed him, he paused at one point to put in a phone order to a nearby liquor store for half a pint of Beefeater gin and potato chips.

(left) "Is That a Grasshopper, Or Is It a Moth?" – Hollywood Bowl, Los Angeles, 1968

(below) Jim the crooner, in the studio, 1968

When writer Bernard Wolfe said that his peers thought of alcohol as "an old-hat ease-giver," Morrison had a ready response.

Jim: My peers are all dopers. Dope's all the go now. Well, I always have to buck the stream. I don't feel right in the majority. The most revolutionary thing you can pump into your system these days in the midst of all these dopers is good old rotgut firewater. Booze is mother's milk to me and better than any milk [that] ever came from any mother.

I hate the kind of sleazy sexual connotations of scoring from people, so I never do that. That's why I like alcohol; you can go down to any corner store or bar and it's right across the table … it's traditional.

Ray: It started with Felix Venable, when Jim moved in with Felix and Phil O'Leno when he was at UCLA. Phil was sort of sane/insane; Felix is gone. They were consuming strange drugs. Belladonna, Asthmador— the Green Lady was making her appearance, and LSD and marijuana, but we all took that. And drinking, that's when the drinking started. Felix was an alcoholic, he was ten years older than Jim, and he died of cirrhosis of the liver.

Ray had another theory about Jim's drinking.

Ray: The stage was Jim's favorite place to be. The last thing he wanted to do was get off the stage. He'd like to stay up there all night if he could. I think that one of the reasons he kept drinking was to keep that high from being on the stage going. We'd leave, and he was still ready to go.

Jim (in late 1970): I went through a period when I drank a lot. I had a lot of pressure hanging over me that I couldn't cope with. I also think drinking is a way to cope with living in a crowded environment, and also a product of boredom. But I enjoy drinking: It loosens people up and stimulates conversation sometimes … It's like gambling somehow. You go out for a night of drinking and you don't know where you're going to end up the next day. It could work out good or it could be disastrous. It's like the throw of the dice.

One such dice toss got him entwined with two fellow rock stars: Jimi Hendrix and Janis Joplin. One night in March 1968, Hendrix was participating in a late-evening jam session at Steve Paul's Scene in

x

(left) Jim in the Afghan vest that Pam gave him, at the Hollywood Bowl, 1968

New York. Reports, as always, vary, but the one in **The Doors On the Road,** *by Greg Shaw, was based on a tape recording.*

"On this night, Hendrix opens the set with a stirring rendition of 'Red House.' He is soon accompanied by an extremely intoxicated Jim Morrison, who staggers onto the stage and proceeds to wail some explicitly obscene lyrics in accompaniment to the band's progression of blues songs.

"As the medley continues, Morrison's condition deteriorates until he collapses into a stupor, after which he leaves the stage ... Paul Caruso (harmonica player) recalls watching Morrison stumble off the stage and proceed to knock over a table full of drinks into Janis Joplin's lap. She sarcastically retaliates by loudly proclaiming, in her long Texan drawl, 'I wouldn't mind ... if he could sing!'"

John: In the beginning, we were like brothers. As time went on it became three and one. It was harder to communicate with Jim. Musically, it was always OK because we didn't talk that much about what we were doing. It was intuitive. But it was hard seeing a friend self-destruct and not being able to stop him. It was the sixties when everything was mellow and you didn't really confront. Now I would take him by the shirt. But I was afraid of him, too. He was very powerful. He was a little older and real smart. When he came into a room, it was, 'Jesus, who is that?' That kind of power. He knew I disapproved of what he was doing. I wouldn't be around or I'd storm out. I never directly said it, though. You didn't do that. But if more people had confronted him, we might have had one less great album, but maybe he would still be around."

Paul Rothchild: Stop him? Everybody tried to stop him! We *all* tried to stop him. We even hired *professionals* to stop him. He was unstoppable.

Robby: Yeah, there was nothing you could do about it. People would tell Jim he should drink less, and Jim would take them out and get them drunk.

PAMELA'S BOUTIQUE

There was preserved in her the fresh miracle of surprise.
—Jim Morrison, writing about Pamela

In late 1967, Ray Manzarek became the first Door to be married—to his Dorothy. He proposed after getting his first Elektra royalty check, and they married on December 21 at city hall, with Jim and Pam serving as best man and bridesmaid. The four celebrated afterward with margaritas and enchiladas on Olivera Street.

After the wedding, Manzarek claims, Pamela was always after Jim to get married. "Jim," she would say, "it was so easy for Ray and Dorothy. Why don't we do it too?" Some say she began calling herself "Mrs. Morrison."

Jim Morrison continued to juggle Pamela with other women. But, by now, Pam was also going off on assignations of her own. The two constantly fought. One popular line of thought had Pam badgering Jim to leave The Doors. He was a poet, not a rock star, she's said to have said. He was a true artist and didn't need the other guys.

Ray: Somehow I could never see Pamela actually saying that. I think that's a myth to make Pamela seem to be a bit of an intellectual. And the last thing in the world Pamela Courson would do is live on a poet's income.

Without his rock 'n' roll money, Morrison certainly wouldn't have been able to help Pam to realize her dream of owning a fashionable boutique.

The store was called Themis—the name of the Greek goddess of justice—and specialized in all that was hip, psychedelic, exotic, elegant, and expensive. Pamela took trips to Europe and Africa to find clothing for the store. But, Penny Courson notes, Pamela didn't rely only on others for her fashions.

Penny Courson: She had a pattern cutter upstairs, and most of the things that were hanging in the shop were things of her own design.

People could come and have their measurements taken and have it made in a different fabric.

She got the idea for Themis in an interesting way. She was a good friend of Slash's mother and father. She babysat him when he was three or four years old, and his mother had a boutique. This is where Pam got the idea. She watched how it was run and learned about it. She was very artistic.

Bill Siddons: I thought it was the most extravagant gift a man could give a woman. And Jim loved giving her the gift. He loved that Pamela was having so much fun with it.

The boutique was a testament to Courson's standing among the many young women who considered themselves potential one-and-onlys of Jim Morrison's.

There really was only one of those.

(below and right) "She Has Robes and She Has Monkeys, Lazy Diamond-Studded Flunkies…"

(below) Orpheus ascending at the Roundhouse, London, 1968

(right) Jim getting ready to record at TT&G studios during the *Waiting for the Sun* sessions, Los Angeles, 1968

7 WAITING FOR THE SUN

7 WAITING FOR THE SUN

Strange Days, released in September 1967, earned some strong reviews. In the L.A. Free Press, Gene Youngblood, who'd praised the debut album, called the new one "a landmark in rock music," noting, "It ventures beyond the conventional realm of musical expression: It has become the theatre." In Circus, Eric Van Lustbader declared Strange Days to be "The Doors' best album" and likened listening to it to "watching Fellini's Satyricon. Morrison's words are so cinematic that each song begins to form pictures in the mind."

The album earned a gold record and reached No. 3 in the Billboard album chart, but its producer considered it a failure.

Paul Rothchild: *Strange Days* was the best album. It said everything we were trying to say musically, and it contains some of Jim's best poetry. It was musically exploratory. It was filled with ingenuity, creativity, great songs, great playing, fabulous singing. Even the cover won all sorts of awards. We all thought it was the best album. Significantly, it was also the one with the weakest sales. We were confident it was going to be bigger than anything The Beatles had done. But, there was no single. The record died on us. It never really *conquered* like it should have.

Nineteen sixty-eight, the hardest of the sixties' many tumultuous years, was no easier on The Doors. They were one of the biggest rock bands in America; their albums were selling well and they were getting concert work, despite their growing reputation as an unreliable and unpredictable act. (The previous December, Morrison registered a no-show in Sacramento, and a second concert at the Shrine in L.A. was stopped by police because of audience misbehavior.)

Also on the positive side of the ledger, Morrison learned that the charges leveled against him in New Haven, Connecticut, had been dropped. But on the business level and in the recording studio, problems lay in wait.

In January, the band entered the T.T.&G. Recording Studios in Hollywood (Sunset Sound was previously booked) to begin their new album. With them came the dreaded "third album syndrome."

Robby: Usually, a group will have enough songs to record one, maybe two albums. Then they'll go off on tour and not have time to write any more material. So by the third album, you find yourself trying to write new songs and having to work them out in the studio—and it shows, usually.

Jim: When we were contracted to provide so many albums a year, so many singles every six months, that natural, spontaneous, generative process wasn't given a chance to happen, as it had in the beginning…

Robby: It got more difficult as time went on, because … well, for one thing, Jim was writing less, and then I would start writing more.

(previous spread) Jim mesmerizes
European audiences on The Doors
'68 tour.

(below) Robby: "Ah, the rock 'n' roll
lifestyle. We played with Jefferson Airplane
and didn't take the stage until three a.m."
London, 1968

left) Jim backstage, New York, 1968

But Morrison, through thick and drunk, continued to write in his notebooks, and the band agreed to devote an entire side of the record to one of Morrison's longer poems, "Celebration of the Lizard."

In the studio, however, a numbing lethargy set in.

Paul Rothchild: Jim was really not interested. He wanted to do other things like write. Being lead singer of The Doors was really not his idea of a good time now. It became very difficult to get him involved with the record.

John: Jim was bringing drug-addict friends to the studio, and it was really dark.

Besides druggies, groupies (both male and female), and assorted hangers-on, who Rothchild would have to kick out, Jim's guests included several buddies from UCLA days who were making a documentary about The Doors, called Feast of Friends. They included Frank Lisciandro, Paul Ferrara, and Babe Hill.

Ray: They were the "Faux Doors." And it was like a battle between "Jimbo" and the Faux Doors and Jim Morrison and the other three Doors. Except those guys never really did anything. I resented them for taking Jim away from his creativity. He would sit in the bar and talk and laugh and talk and laugh. And those guys had nothing better to do than to carouse with Jim, and he was very personable, a great guy to have a beer with.

The Faux Doors were angels compared to some of Morrison's other guests. One night, his guests included a groupie who proceeded to remove her undergarments in the vocal booth and offered herself to all takers. Another evening, a plastered Morrison collapsed on the studio floor and urinated. Fed up, John threw down his drumsticks and left the studio.

John: But I came back the next day. Music is my soul; this is my path. It's with this crazy lead singer, unfortunately, and as painful as it was, I

Unwilling as they were to confront Morrison—who wasn't listening, anyway, the real Doors decided that a babysitter might help. Rothchild knew Bob Neuwirth, a singing, songwriting hipster in New York best known as Bob Dylan's pal and roadie. As Rothchild told Morrison's bandmates, "He can entertain him and deal with him intellectually, out-boogie him, and drink more, run harder, sleep less, and get him to the show on time." With a cover story—that Neuwirth was making a promotional video, alongside the Feast of Friends crew, he would join on tour in March.

One evening, when the three Doors, sans Jim, were at the studio, Joan Didion, then writing for one of the leading mainstream weekly magazines of the day, the Saturday Evening Post, visited. She was with her husband, John Gregory Dunne, a screenwriter who wanted to see Morrison about taking a role in a movie he was producing, The Panic in Needle Park. Didion, meantime, hoped to talk with him for her article.

The Doors, she noted, were nothing like The Beatles. "Their music insists that love is sex and sex is death and therein lives salvation. The Doors are the Norman Mailers of the Top 40, missionaries of apocalyptic sex."

She sat and watched the musicians as they idled away the time, waiting for their tardy lead singer. Her article detailed the bits of conversation she overheard—about LSD and transcendental meditation—and the guys' response when Morrison finally showed up. They said not a word, choosing, instead, to attend to their various instruments. She takes notes as Jim, in his "black vinyl pants" (they were leather) lights a match and lowers it toward his fly.

"It will be some weeks before The Doors finish recording this album," she concluded. "I do not see it through."

Jim: I knew she was gonna do it that way…These chicks, these journalists, if you don't really come on to them, they feel neglected, you know? She ended up doing a number. It was written good, though

John: The article definitely captured the angst and the magic and the weirdness of it. She caught the whole thing in a few pages.

Robby: It took forever, like she said, and mainly because Jim was a little messed up. But that was a time when we came up with some pretty amazing stuff in the studio with Jim being drunk out of his mind. Like "Five to One." That just came one day—"OK, let's try something, do a beat, here's a lick." I don't know whether he had those words first or not. I think that was a poem. He was very good at fitting his poems into music.

The band may not have had much to say to each other, but they were still a band. One day, Morrison told them that it might be time to change managers.

John: The two managers we had, Sal Bonafede and Asher Dann, were trying to convince Jim to go solo, and were trying to dump us. We didn't even know about it. Jim said, "We should fire those guys," and that was really great of Jim. We put this together, all four of us: It was an incredible sweet democracy for several years. Bill Siddons was a trusted roadie—maybe not real experienced, but we were pretty big, and everyone was calling us, so I think it was an excellent move to make him the manager.

The band asked Jac Holzman for an advance, with which they would buy out the remainder of their contract with their managers. Holzman came through. With the new setup came The Doors' first offices, a modest duplex, formerly an antiques store, on Santa Monica Boulevard. Siddons and other staffers had an upstairs office, while the main room was a rehearsal space for the band.

But was Siddons, a twenty-year-old with no music-business experience, the right choice to manage the most popular rock band in America?

John: We had other agents and lawyers, but Bill really did it. He learned how to manage. In fact, after a while, he got this idea of dropping the booking agent, because people would call us direct, so we didn't even have to pay that ten percent commission for a while.

(below) Jim basking in the glow at the
Hollywood Bowl, 1968

(below) Roundhouse, London, 1968

Whether by design or accident, a mini Doors World was forming in West Hollywood, on and around Santa Monica Boulevard and La Cienega. The office was around the corner from Elektra's new recording studio. Also on La Cienega was one of the low-rate motels Morrison camped out at—the Alta Cienega. The office was handy to The Phone Booth, a topless bar Morrison liked to frequent, and a liquor store. Even Pamela's new boutique would only be a short trek away, in the Clear Thoughts Building, on La Cienega.

Jim rented an apartment just a few blocks from the office, on Norton Avenue. It turned out to be just upstairs from Diane Gardiner, a publicist at Rogers, Cowan & Brenner, where she brought in rock acts, including Jefferson Airplane and ... The Doors.

Gardiner was none too pleased about her new neighbor.

Diane: I always had a very hard time with Jim. He wasn't very cooperative, and so that apartment was my haven. One day I was walking back home from the Arrow market and coming towards me was Jim Morrison, and I thought, "Oh dear!" And he said, "Let me take those groceries," and this was a whole other person. He walked me to my door and he said, "You know, I live here now." And I thought, well, here's a nightmare! But it didn't turn out that way.

Soon after the office opened, a new person came onto the scene. He was Danny Sugerman, a teenager who'd recently become a fan through his friendship with Rich Linnell, a friend of Krieger's who helped out as a roadie on occasion. Sugerman attended a Doors concert, got hooked, and showed up at the office, willing to help with anything that might be needed. Soon, Morrison befriended him and gave him a "job"—handling the band's fan mail.

Jim often visited the office, where he had his own desk. Sometimes, when it was just too difficult to find his way to wherever Pam or another girl was, or to one of his motels, he'd sleep in the office.

But The Doors' new hangout didn't make things any better in the recording studio.

(below) John keeping time at the
Roundhouse, London, 1968

For one thing, the band was getting tired—exhausted, even—with Rothchild's perfectionist ways. The producer had taken to demanding multiple takes on songs. "Multiple" actually doesn't adequately describe the situation.

John: The ultimate in indulgence was "The Unknown Soldier." Rothchild had us do 130 takes! It was ludicrous … the heart was lost.

Paul: We got into heavy vocal compositing because Jim would come in too drunk to sing decently. Sometimes we'd put together eight different takes of a song to make one good one.

Rothchild said "Soldier" was a complicated, orchestral number, but another reason that he may have been so meticulous about it was that he was striving, along with the Elektra brass, for another hit single. Since "Light My Fire," The Doors had been whiffing, with "People Are Strange" and "Love Me Two Times."

Robby: This was the only time we actually tried to make a hit single. I remember Paul saying, "We're gonna make a hit this time." We studied the hits of the day and said, "OK, let's see how many beats per minute most of the hits are, and what key they're in," and Paul came up with "Unknown Soldier." That was supposed to be our big hit.

The song did begin with a tempo that reminded of, say, Los Bravos's 1966 hit "Black Is Black." But in the middle was a literally dead stop—for a sequence in which the central soldier got executed by a firing squad.

The scene would be dramatized in concert, with Morrison standing, ramrod straight, as if tied to a pole, and with Krieger "aiming" his guitar at him as if it were a rifle. A loud shot would ring out, and Morrison would crumple, quite convincingly, to the floor.

The Doors also acted out the song in a video—a pioneer effort in those years before MTV—and it was played at their concerts. Television, however, paid scant attention, and when Elektra released "Soldier" as a single in May, while a new album was still in progress, it barely squeezed into the Top 40.

(**below**) Robby, playing chords with
Flamenco flair...

JD: It got to No. 39, which at the time was a miracle, because it was against the war.

Do you know we are being led to slaughters by placid admirals
And that fat slow generals are getting obscene on young blood
     —"An American Prayer"

Robby: We were singing about the revolution. Well, you know, we were never really protagonists of the flower movement. In fact, we were the complete opposite. All these hippies were going, "Oh, love and peace..." But that was only one side of the coin. And we were providing a glimpse of the other side as well.

Jim: I haven't studied politics that much, really. It just seems to me that you have to be in a state of constant revolution, or you're dead. There always has to be a revolution. It has to be a constant thing, not something that's going to change things, and that's it, "the revolution's going to solve everything." It has to be every day.

While "The Unknown Soldier" was out doing battle on the pop charts, the rest of the album was still going through a torturous labor.

"The Celebration of the Lizard" wasn't working out. The band—and Rothchild—couldn't meld its many segments into a cohesive, musical whole, and wound up salvaging only a portion, entitled "Not to Touch the Earth."

That song includes the lines "I am the Lizard King / I can do anything," which would come to haunt Morrison. He was being ironic, he said. But he really was fascinated with things reptilian.

Jim: We must not forget that the lizard and the snake are identified with the unconscious and with the forces of evil. There's something deep in human memory that responds strongly to snakes. Even if you've never seen one. I think that a snake just embodies everything that we fear.

Without "Celebration..." to occupy an entire side of an album, the band had to scramble for more material. One solution was to go back to one of Morrison's first compositions.

"Hello, I Love You" was a deceptively simple-sounding salute to a young woman ("A café au lait Nubian princess," says Ray) he'd spotted and lusted after on the beach in Venice. It was on the demo that the first version of The Doors cut that day at World Pacific, but, in that raw stage, it didn't sound like much more than a jaunty pop tune, with a harmonica rifflet attached to every line.

Now polished and pumped up by Krieger's guitar, it sounded to many like a cop of The Kinks' "All Day and All of the Night."

Robby: That's funny, because we actually stole it from Cream's "Sunshine of Your Love." That was the drumbeat.

Whoever the inspiration was, The Doors would take it to the top of the charts in early August. It had been a year since "Light My Fire."

While some critics dismissed the new hit as a pop ditty, The Doors included another Morrison song that seemed to sound a political note. "Five to One" warned, "The old get old and the young get stronger … they got the guns but we got the numbers."

Ray: This is 1968 America. This is Jim telling it like it is. That's that whole spirit of the new tribe … We're taking over!

A Krieger composition, "Spanish Caravan," was a showcase for his mastery of the flamenco guitar. The bridge, as it turns out, was borrowed from Isaac Albeniz's composition, "Leyenda," a fact that wound up costing him a few pesos when the Albeniz family heard about this late sixties version of sampling.

Another song worked up for the album Waiting for the Sun didn't make the cut. But that didn't stop the band from making that the title of the album.

As they finished the album in May, The Doors said good-bye to Bob Neuwirth. Morrison knew instantly, back in March, that he'd been brought on as a personal nanny, and converted him into just another drinking buddy. Neuwirth did complete a film of "Not to Touch the Earth," from footage shot in Rochester and Boston, but it was never used.

On the home front, Pamela was gone from Norton Avenue; she was off to Morocco, there to shop for goodies for Themis and, while she was there, to see her well-connected friend and occasional lover, Count Jean de Breteuil. This left Jim with … well, just about anyone he wanted.

One day, Morrison showed up at The Doors' office for a band meeting. He silently went to his desk, glanced at some fan mail, pulled a hamburger out of a paper sack, took a bite, and looked at his bandmates and their manager. "I wanna quit," he said.

The room fell into silence. "Why?" Manzarek and Siddons asked. Ray recalls him responding, "I just can't take it anymore."

Manzarek recalled telling Morrison what a good and easy life they had, touring only occasionally and making their music, when Morrison spoke up again. "I think I'm having a nervous breakdown."

Ray: He suggested that we "get another singer." I countered with a proposal. "Let's give it six months. If you feel the same way then, we'll break the band up."

"OK, six months," he said. He asked our secretary, Kathy Lisciandro, not to call him for a couple of days, and left.

John: Ray pressed this band to play a year longer than we should have. Jim was destroying himself.

Krieger had heard it all before.

Robby: He would say stuff like that all the time. It just depended on his mood at the time. It was like the night up at the house when he was going to kill himself. So you never could believe what Jim was saying seriously when he said stuff like that.

Especially when The Doors were about to hit the road again—this time with major concerts in New York, Europe, and, first of all, the fabled Hollywood Bowl.

(left) Robby, snarling onstage at the Hollywood Bowl, Los Angeles, 1968.

(below) Jim bums a smoke from someone in the audience at the Hollywood Bowl, 1968

This was a special hometown gig. The Bowl, opened in 1922, was the home of "music under the stars" with the L.A. Philharmonic. KHJ, "Boss Radio," the ruling Top-40 station in town, was presenting The Doors, along with Steppenwolf and The Chambers Brothers who, not all that long ago, had shared the Whisky a Go Go stage with their opening act, The Doors.

The Feast of Friends film crew was on hand. Oh—and so was Mick Jagger. Having completed The Stones' latest album, Beggar's Banquet, Mick, along with Marianne Faithfull, had flown in. His band was about to tackle larger arenas, like The Doors, and he wanted to check out the show.

On the afternoon of the concert, July 5, 1968, Jagger found Morrison at the Alta Cienega and paid a short visit, talking about the challenges of playing to big crowds. Meantime, The Doors' crew loaded up the Bowl stage with fifty-four amplifiers, capable of blasting sixty thousand watts of rock power a mile away.

The stage was set.

Unfortunately, Jim Morrison didn't show. Actually, he did—but it wasn't the Morrison rock fans had come to expect: the unpredictable shaman madman. Perhaps it was the Hollywood Bowl. It might have been the knowledge that Mick Jagger was in the audience, along with Faithfull, Stones producer Jimmy Miller, and, sitting close by, the lovely Pamela Courson.

Whatever the reason, he chose to just stand there and sing, one song after another. He recited from his lizard opus, drawing cries from the audience for "Light My Fire." He talked back to them, but he also charmed them with jokes and poetry. Mostly, though, he sang, and The Doors delivered a solid performance. It just wasn't a spectacle, and Morrison had taught Jagger nothing about handling a large concert space.

John: We went out onstage to eighteen thousand roaring people. I wanted to show The Stones' lead singer how good we could be. Not tonight. Dammit! I wished we were better. Several close friends were right in the front seats and I couldn't even look at them. Jim wore a

(below) Jim (right), doing the two-step as Robby plays at the Hollywood Bowl, Los Angeles, 1968

cross and smoked a lot of cigarettes, which seemed out of character for him...I detected some self-conscious image-building.

I couldn't put my finger on what went wrong. The lights were very bright for the film crew, and I could tell they were affecting Jim's performance. The mood of the show wasn't there. We didn't have enough power and Jim's pauses were too long on some songs.

"What went wrong?" I asked Robby, walking back under the shell to the dressing rooms.

"Jim took acid right before going on."

"GODDAMMIT!" I hurled my drumsticks to the floor. "It's one thing to take it on your own time, but the Hollywood Bowl?"

Later Jagger was very kind when *Melody Maker,* the English music magazine, asked him how he liked The Doors. He said, "They were nice chaps, but they played a bit too long."

(below) Waiting for The Who to get
offstage …

(below) Jim writhing onstage at the Westbury Music Fair, New York, 1969

(following page left) Jim leaning on Robby's guitar amps, London, 1968

(following page right) Jim lifting the crowd with him at the Santa Clara Music Festival, 1968

(below) Jim getting it on in 1969 on the East Coast

"I don't think the shaman, from what I've read, is really too interested in defining his role in society. He's just interested in pursuing his own fantasies. If he became too self-conscious of a function, I think it might tend to ruin his own inner trip."
—Jim Morrison, 1969

8 "IT'S FUN BEING ONSTAGE"

8 "IT'S FUN BEING ONSTAGE"

"All right, now look, look…You've got to sit down; you've got to move back to your seats; you've got to make aisles, or that's it. You've got to move back. I want everyone to get back to their seats. People are going to get hurt up here. They're going to pass out. And we don't want it. And The Doors don't want it either."

—Unidentified announcer at a Doors concert

What The Doors wanted was to challenge the status quo in whatever they did, on recordings or in concert. Morrison, who began, after all, by jumping onstage with Rick and the Ravens to shout out "Louie Louie" and by faking being a guitarist at his first paid "gig," didn't buy the standard artist-to-audience relationship.

Jim: I see it as more than performing, going on, doing songs and leaving. I take everything personally, and don't really feel I've done a complete job unless we've gotten everybody in the theater on a common ground.

I always try to get them to stand up, to feel free to move around anywhere they want to. I like people to be free, not chained.

There are no rules at a rock concert. Anything is possible.

Unfortunately, concert promoters, owners, and managers of theaters and other concert venues, and law enforcement officials did have rules, and, as The Doors' concerts became more theatrical, more dramatic, and more provocative, and as audiences increasingly responded to the lead singer as an icon or a sex idol more than as a purveyor of songs, things began to get out of hand.

The fact that The Doors were being followed on the road by the film crew for the Feast of Friends *documentary didn't help matters. Morrison was clearly playing to the cameras and stirring audiences up.*

The first riot—actually, it was a near-riot—had taken place back in May, when the band was playing Chicago for the first time. Morrison encouraged the crowd of some four thousand fans to move closer to the stage, despite police barricades. The Doors performed an incendiary set and made their exit. When the lights came on, some audience members continued to party, one fan jumping from the balcony into the crowd below. Some fans made another move toward the stage, but were held back by cops. The Doors did not return for an encore, and the audience dispersed peacefully.

That would not be the case in August, when The Doors topped the bill of a mini–rock festival in Flushing Meadows, in the borough of Queens, New York. On a humid summer night, a crowd of some seventeen thousand gathered at the Singer Bowl to see The Doors, with an unknown band, Kangaroo, and a well-known one, The Who, opening. The crowd didn't care about Kangaroo, and The Who's set was ruined by a faulty revolving stage, which put the British band out of the sight line of a good portion of the audience. An hour's delay before The Doors hit the stage didn't exactly pep up the crowd.

(previous spread) The Doors rock
Cleveland, 1968

(**left**) Recording a video for "Hello, I Love You" in Frankfurt, 1968

The part of the crowd that could see the band had to look through a phalanx of about twenty New York cops, lined up along the front of the stage. Morrison had to make his way between them to face the audience, which immediately rushed the stage.

The Doors proceeded to play a strong show, with Morrison pulling out all the stops, doing his tightrope walk, collapsing, screaming at the audience, and puzzling them with long readings from "Celebration of the Lizard." Fights broke out; at one point, one patron heaved a chair onto the stage. Morrison tossed it back. Some fans rushed onto the stage, only to be thrown off.

Robby: Our roadie, Vince Treanor, loved shoving people off the stage.

Ray: And the more you shoved them the more the people would come onto the stage.

Robby: Well, it's fun being onstage.

After The Doors got to, and through, "The End," and fled backstage, the excited crowd, many of whom had helped Morrison with his Oedipal recital at the song's climax, went crazy, wrecking the seating section in front of the stage and charging the police barricade.

Later, backstage, the film crew caught Jim sitting on a bench with a teenage girl who had been injured by a flying chair. He brushed her hair and tried to soothe her. "She was just an innocent bystander," he says. "It's a democracy."

In his book, John Densmore wrote that "The Doors never really had any riots ... I mean a riot's an out-of-control, violent thing. We never had too much of what I call a real riot."

Robby Krieger believes that Singer Bowl was not exactly a tea party.

Robby: I would say that qualifies as a riot. And also Cleveland, the next night. They did the same thing; they just destroyed every chair in

But after a few calmer concerts around the East Coast, The Doors packed up. It was time for "the American Rolling Stones," as they were beginning to be called, to go to Europe.

"WHAT'RE YOU DOING HERE?"

In the fall of 1968, The Doors and Jefferson Airplane were booked for concerts together in Stockholm, Copenhagen, London, Hamburg, Düsseldorf, and Amsterdam. The bands, who the media played up as rock rivals, would take turns opening for each other.

Grace Slick, the so-called "Acid Queen" of the San Francisco rock scene of the sixties, could match Jim Morrison drink for drink. In her memoir, *Somebody to Love?*, she recalled walking around downtown Holland one afternoon with her fellow Airplane, Paul Kantner, and The Doors, and getting recognized by fans.

Grace: They'd come up and talk, handing us various drugs as gifts of thanks for our music. Most of us just said "Thank you," and put whatever it was in our pockets for later. Jim, on the other hand, stopped, sat down on the curb, and did it right up. Pot, hash, coke—whatever. I thought he was ingesting an overly interesting combination of chemicals for that night's concert.

She was right. At the Concertgebouw, the Airplane opened the show and were playing "Plastic Fantastic Lover" when Morrison suddenly appeared onstage. He began doing one of his drunken, druggy dervish dances, and the Airplane, amused at the sight of their surprise guest star, revved up the song, sending Morrison twirling around until his legs got tangled among guitar cables. He fell, got up, danced some more, took a bow, and retreated backstage.

Ray: He leans up against the wall in the dressing room and very slowly, with a beer in his hand, slides down the wall and passes out. And that was it. He was gone.

The paramedics loaded him onto a stretcher and carried him out into an ambulance. We played our set without him, and Robby and I sang

8 "IT'S FUN BEING ONSTAGE"

(below) Ray and Jim having a cold one on the streets of Frankfurt after performing, 1968

Manzarek, Krieger, and Densmore did fine, beginning with a rousing "Break On Through" and concluding with "The Unknown Soldier." The next day, the Amsterdam paper ran a front-page photo of The Doors, focusing on ... John Densmore.

John: I felt pretty good about that, like, "Check this out, Jim." You know, Ray sang, we did our thing, and it wasn't the same, but we were tight, we were a good band.

The European tour—which included performances for television stations in West Germany and Copenhagen—concluded without incident, and The Doors and their crew flew back to Los Angeles. Except for Jim Morrison. Pamela Courson had flown to London with him and had stayed there while The Doors toured. Now, he rejoined her at a flat she'd found in the upscale Belgravia area. There, they watched a television special produced by Granada, which had tracked them from customs through their first concert at the Round House in London. Later, they were joined by Michael McClure, a famed Beat era poet who'd befriended Morrison and wanted to talk about a film project. McClure also encouraged Jim to publish the poetry he'd been compiling in his notebooks for years.

Morrison didn't maintain contact with the home office, and, while he was gone, The Doors got an offer that tested their equal-partners rule, which required all four to agree on a decision before a project could go forward.

Bill Siddons: Jim had decided to disappear. For four days no one had any idea where he was and suddenly Buick was offering close to a hundred thousand dollars to use "Light My Fire" in a commercial. It was going to be "Come on, Buick, Light My Fire."

Since Robby was the actual writer of the song, I felt he should make the decision. For some reason it was a high pressure, "You gotta give an answer now" situation, so together we all decided, "Well, what the hell ... why not?" You know, we were all practically teenagers.

And Jim came back in a couple of days and just freaked out. He thought it was the tackiest thing in the world to do with The Doors' music.

According to Manzarek, who thought of the commercial as a harmless bit of additional television exposure for The Doors as well as a welcome infusion of cash, Morrison got the commercial stopped. But Siddons says that Morrison's protests came too late, and that the commercials were aired a few times in a few parts of the country.

Despite their disagreement, the band continued to take care of business. They had to begin a new album. They got a look at the footage for Feast of Friends and agreed that the film needed more work. The band voted to allot a few thousand more dollars to get the film completed, with editor Frank Lisciandro working out of The Doors' offices. And they had an appearance to do on The Smothers Brothers Comedy Hour.

For this show, hosted by the comic folk duo with a decidedly liberal, antiwar, pro-marijuana bent, Morrison not only showed up; he looked the best he had in many months. A beard he had grown in recent months was shaven; his hair was long and flowing, shades of the Jay Sebring–style of his early haircuts, and he looked aglow in a dark blue shirt and his black leather pants.

He was not only the star; he was the only musician actually performing. The music for "Touch Me" had already been laid down, and the rest of The Doors, featured sax player Curtis Amy, and the Smothers show's orchestra, would all be feigning their parts.

Jim was live, and acquitted himself well, although he missed his re-entry on the second chorus by a few "Come on's."

Krieger, who appeared on the show with a whopping black (left) eye, previously explained it away as the result of a fight with some rednecks. "I was protecting Jim from some bad guys," he said. Now, he admits, he told that tale "because it sounded better. It actually was an auto accident."

The Doors concluded the year with a concert at the Forum, which, in 1968, was the largest venue available for a rock concert in the Los Angeles area. Among the eighteen thousand or so in the audience was one Andy Morrison. In 1968, he was nineteen and a college student who was only too happy to have the chance to party with his rock-star brother.

Andy: We started out over at The Doors office and the limo came. Across the street there's a liquor store, and I got a six pack of beer and he got a pint of vodka. The other guys were inside and we were out in the parking lot, so I get about two or three beers down and he drinks the whole pint of vodka and a couple of beers and breaks the bottle on a brick wall back there, and we jumped in the limousine and we both stayed up front with the limo driver. It was like Jim and the rest of the guys were on a different page. We drive in, and there's people in the parking lot and they come running up and beat on the windows, waving at him.

It was the first concert where they had guys in tuxedos with the violin section, and people listened to that a bit, then they said they'd had enough of that shit and everybody started yelling "Light My Fire." There was a big guy with a beard playing the saxophone and I told Jim later, "It just didn't look right, this guy was up there with The Doors playing the saxophone, and between his licks, he was just looking at the audience, grinning and having a good time, and he didn't fit in with the rest of the guys."

Afterward they had a party somewhere in the building. Then Jim and Pam and I went out and we played invisible soccer ball in the parking lot for a while and went home.

Andy did not seem to recall that his brother was particularly bellicose that night, especially in response to those inevitable calls for "Light My Fire."

After performing the song, he sat down on the stage and addressed the audience. "What're you doing here?" he asked. "Why did you come tonight?" When the crowd grew suddenly reticent, he continued: "Well, man, we can play music all night, but that's not what you really want, is it? You want something else, something more, something greater than you've ever seen before. Right?"

The crowd roared, and Morrison spat back: "Well, fuck you. We came to play music."

And with that, The Doors rolled into a long version of "Celebration of the Lizard," leaving most of the audience dazzled, dazed, and silent as they filed out of the Forum.

8 "IT'S FUN BEING ONSTAGE"

(below) John and Ray digging in at the
Roundhouse, London, 1968.

8 "IT'S FUN BEING ONSTAGE"

(below) Jim doing the Shaman's dance

(below) Ray in the Shaman's trance

(below and right) Robby and John getting it on … making the Shaman prance … at the Roundhouse, London, 1968

9 MAYHEM IN MIAMI

9 MAYHEM IN MIAMI

Jim: I think that was the culmination, in a way, of our mass performing career. Subconsciously, I think I was trying to get across in that concert—I was trying to reduce it to absurdity, and it worked too well. I was just fed up with the image that had been created around me … It just got too much for me to really stomach, and so I just put an end to it in one glorious evening.

Robby: He really didn't do anything that wrong, except being too drunk and doing a bad show. But it ruined our career for at least a year, and probably was one of the contributing factors to the demise of The Doors.

Bill Siddons: The Miami concert was pretty much the end of The Doors as we knew them.

The Miami concert, arrest, trial, and verdict did not, in fact, bring an end to The Doors. They produced two more studio albums—two of their best efforts, in fact—and performed more concerts. But, whether or not the other Doors knew it, Morrison was ready to move on. As he told me:

Jim: I think there's a certain moment when you're right in time with your audience and then you both grow out of it, and you just have to realize that it's not that you have outgrown the audience, it's just that the audience and you both are too old for that. That has to go on something else, and let the younger people do that.

But, there were a number of other contributing factors to the personal and professional debacle that was the concert that evening of March 1, 1969, at the Dinner Key Auditorium at the Coconut Grove.

First, there was Jim's mental state and his anguish over being a sex-idol puppet, his interest in testing audiences and conventional limits; his concern that his time in the spotlight had passed, his interest in other art forms. As he told a classical music composer he'd recently met in New York, "If I don't find a new way to develop creatively within a year, I'll be good for nothing but nostalgia."

Second, there was his physical state. He missed two flights on his way from Los Angeles to Miami and drank while waiting for planes in L.A. and New Orleans. And, of course, he drank on board as well. And on arrival backstage, too—why not?

Third, there was his recent immersion into the art of confrontational theatre. His friend Michael McClure had hipped him to The Living Theatre, a thirty-two-person troupe that was touring the United States with various productions, including one called Paradise Now. Morrison bought tickets for their shows in San Francisco and Los Angeles and paid rapt attention as the performers engaged the audience in dialogue and raged about the rules of society, rules that kept them out of Paradise.

"I'm not allowed to take my clothes off!" one actor screamed. As others spoke about how "the culture represses love," they began taking their clothes off, stripping to their underwear.

(previous spread) Two of Jim's pensive moments captured in a unique photo overlay. Dinner Key Auditorium, Miami, 1969.

(below) Ray: "Jim with his sweet little lamb. I remember him saying, 'This thing is so cute, who would want to eat it?'" The hat and the lamb were given to Jim by animal-rights activist Lou Marvin prior to the show in Miami, 1969

9 MAYHEM IN MIAMI

(below) Jim, totally possessed in Miami,
1969

Morrison joined the audience in participating in various performances. At the end of one evening, Tom Baker said Jim turned to him and said, "Let's start a fire in the balcony or something. Get a riot going."

There was also the matter of the time and place of the Miami concert. Nineteen sixty-eight had been a hard, hard year for those who wanted an end to the war and get a friendly, progressive figure in the White House. They got an escalation—and Richard M. Nixon. Young people were in a feisty, fighting mood.

As for choosing to personalize his Living Theatre experiences in Miami, as former Doors manager Bill Siddons put it: "He didn't do it for prurient reasons. It was theatre. But it happened in Florida, a real black-and-white state, and it was the South."

Add to that the situation at the Dinner Key Auditorium itself: The promoter, Siddons claimed, oversold the venue, paying The Doors for the theater's six thousand capacity, but selling more than ten thousand tickets.

Bill Siddons: You ever seen sardines in a can? They have a lot of room compared to what that place was like that night. There was no air-conditioning, and it was one of the hottest nights of the year.

The show started late, and then it got later, as Morrison spent his first few minutes onstage noodling on a harmonica and talking to the crowd up front, asking if anyone had anything to drink. The other Doors began "Break On Through," but Morrison was in no mood to sing. Instead, he began talking/preaching in an exaggerated accent of no particular derivation.

Jim: I ain't talkin' about no revo-LU-shon,
And I'm not talkin' about no demon-STRAY-shon
I'm talkin' about having a good time!

Robby: Oh, it was just total chaos. First of all, he was wasted—drunk—and he was just storming around the stage, screaming and yelling, and we were trying to play as we often did, trying to keep it together, the three of us, by playing songs and hitting different cues that he would spontaneously come up with something on. But even those weren't

working that night because the audience was just yelling and screaming back, and he was just yelling and screaming back.

Jim: You're all a bunch of fucking idiots.

How long are you gonna let 'em push you around.

You love it. You're all a bunch of slaves, bunch of slaves.

What are you gonna do about it? What are you gonna do about it? What are you gonna do about it? What are you gonna do?

It was a vitriolic mix of confrontational theatre and Mario Savio, the Free Speech Movement firebrand who rallied protesters at UC Berkeley.

He referenced The Living Theatre as he shrugged off the band's attempt to get him into "When the Music's Over," speaking, instead. "I used to think the whole thing was a joke," he said. "I used to think it was something to laugh about. And then the last couple of nights I met some people who were doing something. They're trying to change the world, and I want to get on the trip."

Morrison wandered off into a bit of a song, and then returned to his rant, telling the audience, "I want to see you have some fun...no limits, no laws!"

The band tried "Light My Fire." Morrison grabbed his crotch. When someone drenched him with champagne, he began taking off his shirt, as the audience roared. "Let's see a little skin," Morrison said. "Let's get naked." Members of the audience began undressing.

Bill Siddons: The audience wanted their show, goddamn it! But he was taunting the audience, going, "What are you here for? Is this what you came to see?" And he was pointing to his dick. "I mean, what do you want from me?" It was the first time I heard him being completely confrontational with his audience, instead of just being provocative.

John: Then Jim hinted that he was going to strip all the way. "You didn't come here for music. You came for something else. Something greater

9 MAYHEM IN MIAMI

than you've ever seen." Ray yelled at Vince Treanor, our equipment chief, to stop him.

Vince: Ray says, "Vince, don't let him take his pants down." I went right out and got behind Jim and put my fingers into his belt loops and twisted them so he couldn't unbuckle them, if he was going to.

Jim: Hey, listen, I'm lonely. I need some love, you all.

Ain't nobody gonna love my ass? C'mon, I need ya.

There are so many of ya out there; nobody's gonna love me?

Sweetheart, c'mon.

Hey, there's a bunch of people back there that I didn't even notice.

Hey, how about about fifty or sixty of you people come up here and love my ass.

Yeah! I love ya! C'mon!

Bill Siddons: The whole thing turned into pandemonium. There were kids jumping all over the stage. All of a sudden, there were police on the stage, throwing the kids off. The promoter's brother was a karate expert; there was all this craziness going on.

John: I decided to bail. As I jumped off the stage and accidentally landed on the light board, which fell to the ground, a security guard flipped Jim like a black-belt karate expert, head over heels into the audience, thinking he was a fan.

Robby and I ran up the stairs to get out of the chaos. Jim was now in the middle of the auditorium, leading a snake dance with ten thousand people following him. I looked down from the balcony, and the audience looked like a giant whirlpool, with Jim at the center.

Ten minutes later the Lizard King strolled into the dressing room with a group of people laughing and talking.

The show was over. For everything that had gone down, there had been no actual riot; no busting of heads; no arrests.

Robby: Everybody had a good time. After the show the cops came up and had some beer with us. If something had happened we would've been arrested. It wasn't till a week later that the charges were brought. What happened was the press got hold of the thing, and they said, "Well, he whipped it out," or something, which he didn't. If he did, believe me, somebody would've snapped a shot of that. It wasn't that easy to miss!

*The press included one reporter at the **Miami Herald**, a young man about Morrison's age and, like him, a former Florida State student. He wrote that Morrison had been obscene, exposed himself, and tried to incite a riot, and called various officials asking why he hadn't been arrested. Four days after the concert, with the local police, city politicians, and state lawmakers all riled up, the Miami police issued an arrest warrant. The charges included a felony (lewd and lascivious behavior, including self-exposure, feigning oral copulation, and feigning masturbation) and three misdemeanors (public drunkenness, profanity, and indecent exposure).*

The charge of "feigning oral copulation" was ludicrous.

Ray: That was Jim on his knees in front of Robby's guitar as Robby played a solo in "Five to One." Jim was feigning worshiping Robby's dexterous fingers as they flew over the fretboard.

*As for self-exposure: That claim would haunt Morrison to his grave. He joked about it, hinting that he might have done it. **Rolling Stone** quoted Bill Siddons saying that, as he left the stage, Morrison said something like, "Uh-oh—I think I exposed myself." Later, he told Ray that he was too drunk to remember what he did—or didn't do. But even if he had, so what? As he reasoned to a reporter, "Six guys and girls are naked every night in **Hair** (the Broadway musical, which was playing in Miami) and nobody calls the cops. My audience expects me to do something freaky. If I'd been in L.A. or New York, nothing would have happened." Donald Bierman, one of his lawyers, said, "I think he feigned exposing himself. Manzarek saw Morrison toying with the shirt he'd removed.*

(left) The Aquarius Theatre, Los Angeles, 1969

(below) View from the stage at The Aquarius Theatre, 1969

Ray: He said, "Well, what can I do? You want to see something, don't you? What can I show you?" He placed the microphone on its stand and held the shirt in front of his crotch. He had the idea. He was going to top The Living Theatre. "How about if I show you my cock?" And he began fumbling behind his shirt, as if he were opening his button fly. No one could see a thing. His shirt covered everything. "OK, I'm gonna show it to you." And he fumbled some more and appeared to take it out of his pants. And then he took the shirt in both hands, holding it like a bullfighter's cape in front of his groin. "OK, watch now … here it comes!" And he pulled the shirt/cape quickly aside—swish—and then back in place. "Did you see it? Did you see my cock?" The shirt was whipped away and then back in place, concealing everything. Exposing nothing.

But by the time the arrest warrants came, there were other forces at work. The FBI, acting on a tip from an informant, filed a report on the Miami concert. Later in March, the FBI charged Morrison with unlawful flight, even though The Doors had planned a Caribbean vacation well before the concert, and no warrant was issued until they were on the islands of Guadalupe and Jamaica.

BANNED IN AMERICA

According to the media of the day, Jim Morrison was guilty until proven innocent. Miami was the first of a planned twenty-city tour. Now, the cancellations poured into The Doors' office.

John: The hall managers had a magazine, and they said don't book this band, and most people thought we were just over the top, too much, the Orange Bowl rally, thirty thousand people got together for decency after we performed and Jackie Gleason and homophobic Anita Bryant manned the rally and Nixon said a congratulations thing to them.

Robby: And they banned our records; most Top 40 stations wouldn't touch it. Maybe some underground stations, too.

Bill Siddons: It cost us at least a half million dollars and almost caused the group to break up. It really destroyed our morale. What we considered a minor incident turned into a tremendous problem.

Still, we were able to work. We kept booking a weekend here and there.

John: You know, I was pleased that all the gigs were canceled after Miami. I couldn't stop this train alone. I was the caboose. The drummer's in the back, and Jim's the engine, and Ray's right behind him shoveling coal in to go forward and faster, and I'm going, *"Where are the brakes?! It's a runaway train."* And when Miami happened, and he did not expose himself, of course, but he was completely ripped and riled everybody up, I went "Great, we're gonna get a break; we need a break. We can record, but, live? This brilliant band is starting to look like shit."

Robby did not blame Morrison for the loss of income caused by Miami. If it hadn't been for Jim, he reasoned, none of them would have been in the position to lose that kind of money.

THE SOFT PARADE

The numerous concert cancellations gave The Doors time for other activities, including the completion of **The Soft Parade,** *which they'd begun in late 1968. Those sessions allowed Elektra to issue a new single to follow the hit, "Hello, I Love You." "Touch Me" reached No. 3 early in 1969 and served to signal a new sound from The Doors: horns and strings.*

Ray: The horns and strings were my idea. It was time; we had done three albums as the small group. We can't do the same thing *again,* for God's sake. And that's what you did, you did an album with horns and strings, you got some jazz and you got some classical and you got some country and western in there. We just put in that lush sound, you've got that hard-rock band, and then, in "Touch Me," the strings come in with "I'm gonna love you," and then the horns come in, playing a bossa nova. I worked with Paul Harris and told him what I wanted and he scored the whole thing and put in a whole bunch of good stuff on his own. So if it didn't work out, it's my fault. But *The Soft Parade* is Doors music just like all the other albums. We just brought in a little whipped cream to put over the top.

John: When we first met, we shared our enthusiasm for Miles Davis and Coltrane and the whole jazz world. We said in rehearsals, before the first album, "Hey, someday, we can add horns, just for fun. We got this sax player, Curtis Amy, for "Touch Me" and told him to play like Coltrane or Archie Shepp and just lose it. We had a real good time. And we got a lot of flack for it. But "Touch Me" was a hit.

As it was with **Waiting for the Sun,** *The Doors had a dearth of material, and the sessions were difficult.*

Paul Rothchild: Jim was really not interested after about the third album. It became very difficult to get him involved with the records. When we made *The Soft Parade,* it was like pulling teeth to get Jim into it.

Jim: It got out of control and took too long in the making. It spread over nine months. An album should be like a book of stories strung together, with some kind of unified feeling and style about it, and that's what *The Soft Parade* lacks.

Robby: The strings and the horns were Paul's idea. I'd like to re-release that album without any of the horns or strings.

The album's title track was a pastiche of different poems of Morrison's, beginning with his observations of the people he saw streaming along Sunset Boulevard in Hollywood.

John: My interpretation of that was the peace movement. "The soft parade has now begun, listen to its engines hum, people out having fun"—you know, trying to change, get off the war machine.

Paul: Whenever we got stuck in the studio with a bridge section, I'd ask Jim to get out his notebooks of poetry, and we'd go through them and find a piece that fit rhythmically and conceptually. A lot of the fragments there were just bits of poetry we put together. That song came out kind of interesting, I thought."

(below) Paul and Ray in the studio
recording *The Soft Parade*, Los Angeles,
1969

The Soft Parade marked a departure from the band's policy of crediting all songs to the entire band. Now, songs bore credits for Morrison, Krieger, or both. It's true that, as Morrison's lyrical output declined along with his interest, Krieger stepped up with more songs, including "Touch Me." But it wasn't a matter of Morrison wanting to give the guitarist due credit. He didn't like a line in Krieger's song, "Tell All the People," which went, "Can't you see me growing, get your guns." As Robby recalls, "He was afraid of people coming to our shows with guns."

The Soft Parade was released in July. With the Miami clouds still hovering over them, the album didn't come close to matching Waiting for the Sun, which was No. 1 for a month. The Soft Parade didn't reach the Top Five, but it still earned the band its fourth consecutive gold album. Reviews were mixed, but the jazzier sound found favor with Jazz & Pop magazine, which said that "none of it is bad, most of it is very superior music, and some of it is absolutely glorious."

The reviewer was Patricia Kennealy, an editorial assistant at the small, New York–based magazine. She had met Morrison in January at The Plaza hotel in Manhattan for an interview. Years later, she would write, in her book, that by May, "I am absolutely certain I am crazy about him."

Paul Rothchild was right about Morrison being distracted by other interests. In March, the film his buddies made, Feast of Friends, was completed to the band's satisfaction. In its own jittery way, it captured the riotous levels that Doors concerts had reached, along with some amusing backstage scenes, and Morrison wanted to do more moviemaking.

Jim: Well, I guess that's what I've always really wanted to do even more than being in a band was to work in films, and I'd like to write and direct a film of my own.

Now, with the help of attorney Max Fink, he set up a film production company and rented an office in the Clear Thoughts Building, where Pamela's boutique was also located. There, his crew, including

(left) Between recording sessions at the Forum, Los Angeles, 1969

(below) Jim "praying to the muse," Los Angeles, 1969

Lisciandro, Paul Ferrara, and Babe Hill could work on his screenplay, tentatively titled **Hitchhiker.** *(Later, it'd evolve into* **Hiway** *and, finally,* **HWY.***)*

Jim: Essentially, there's no plot, no story in the traditional sense. A person, played by me, comes down out of the mountains and hitchhikes his way through the desert into a modern city, which happened to be L.A., and that's where it ends.

While they began shooting around Palm Springs and California's high desert country, Morrison was also engaged with his poetry. He took his notebooks into a recording studio and, with John Haeny, Elektra Records' chief engineer, at the controls, recorded an hour's worth of his works, occasionally singing some of his writing, a cappella. He planned on adding sound effects at a later date, and he hoped that Elektra might release a poetry album down the line, preferably under the name he preferred as a poet: James Douglas Morrison.

With the encouragement he'd received from Michael McClure, he published private volumes of **The Lords**—*random notes and thoughts about vision and cinematography, dating back to his times at UCLA— and* **The New Creatures**—*a selection of more recent poetry, much of it concerned with violence, pain, and death. He published only a hundred copies of each and kept them at The Doors' office, where he would give them away to friends and fans, as he saw fit. The two slim volumes (*The Lords *was actually unbound, comprising of eighty-two loose sheets in a box) would be published as a book in April 1970 by Simon & Schuster. It would be a proud moment for Morrison.*

Jim: Listen, real poetry doesn't say anything, it just ticks off the possibilities. Opens all doors. You can walk through any one that suits you.

…Poetry (is) eternal. As long as there are people, they can remember words and combinations of words. Nothing else can survive a holocaust but poetry and songs. No one can remember an entire novel. No one can describe a film, a piece of sculpture, a painting, but so long as there are human beings, songs and poetry can continue.

If my poetry aims to achieve anything, it's to deliver people from the limited ways in which they see and feel.

Without many concerts lined up, The Doors planned a performance in July at the Aquarius Theater in Hollywood as part of a series of summer shows staged by Elektra Records, to be recorded for a live album. By all reports, The Doors performed well, with Morrison, now fully bearded, chatting amiably with the audience. "For a long time we've wanted to record a live album," he said. "Tonight's the night…Ready? Let's go!"

The performance earned The Doors something they hadn't enjoyed in some time: rave reviews. The Los Angeles Herald-Examiner called them "an assertive, demanding group. They preach revolution. They reach out for love. They play beautiful rock 'n' roll. Robby Krieger is a brilliant, eclectic, and often volcanic guitarist. The Krieger-Manzarek-Densmore instrumental passages are among the most intelligently conceived in contemporary popular music. As an encore—or perhaps as an afterthought—Morrison performed one of his tortured paranoid poems set to music. He slowly left the stage, telling the audience to 'retire now to your dreams.' And what dreams The Doors inspire. They are controlled, compressed nightmares."

The Doors went on to play a couple of rock festivals, one in Eugene, Oregon, another just outside Seattle. But, oddly, come mid-August and what would turn out to be the mother of all mega-rock festivals, near Woodstock, New York, The Doors would be missing from the enormous and eclectic roster of artists.

Ray Manzarek said he voted against going because The Doors no longer wanted to play outdoor concerts. Manager Siddons recalls an entirely different reason for The Doors' absence.

Bill: Our policy had always been: "The Doors headline." They don't play in multiple act bills. And be part of an event. They're an event in and of themselves. But I thought that Woodstock warranted a change in the policy, and so did Jac Holzman, who came over to the office and put his two cents in. And Bill Graham lobbied them too. But the band didn't want to do it.

They just felt they'd be one of many.

The band would soon learn what they missed. Actually, Densmore went with his girlfriend, Julia Negron. They wound up catching a helicopter ride with concert lighting wizard Chip Monck and wound up on one side of the main stage.

John: I stole a glimpse of the audience. *This was it!* A sea of faces cresting at the top of a hill about a quarter of a mile away. The biggest gig ever, and The Doors weren't even playing! Oh, well. I was there.

Ray: Once you saw the film and they said 750,000 hippies attend and you see the aerial shots I thought, "Oh, shit…" The only consolation was, I thought, if we had been there it would have rained on us. Jim would have been electrocuted or Robby, or they would have electrocuted each other.

And so The Doors were absent at the biggest party of the sixties, a decade they had come to represent as well as any other band. But on that historical weekend in the middle of August, Jim Morrison was hiking through the California desert near Palm Springs with a few of his drinking and filmmaking buddies. Woodstock—and rock music—were a world away.

(below) In Mexico for a gig at the Forum, Mexico City, 1969

(right) Jim at the pyramids in Teotihuacán, Mexico 1969

10 ROCK JUSTICE

10 ROCK JUSTICE

Back in the real world, Jim Morrison got right back into trouble. Having been out on bail in the Miami incident, he returned on November 9, 1969 to enter a formal plea of not guilty. Trial was set for April. If convicted, he would face more than three years in Raiford Penitentiary, one of Florida's toughest prisons.

Not even two days later, he was arrested again. He and one of his drinking pals, the actor Tom Baker, along with Frank Lisciandro and Leon Bernard, who was in charge of publicity for The Doors, flew to Phoenix, Arizona, to catch a Rolling Stones concert.

Aboard their Continental Airlines flight, in their first-class section seats, they began—or, more likely, continued—to drink. According to witnesses, Baker got rowdy, yelling at the attendants to fetch drinks more quickly, and, later, throwing peanuts at them. Jim laughed at Baker's antics, but didn't do much else. After Baker allegedly touched one of the women, she told the captain, who issued a warning to the men. Baker continued to be a pain, and when the plane landed, he and Morrison were taken into custody by Phoenix police and charged with public drunkenness and "interfering with a flight crew"—a felony. They spent the night in jail, were released on bail, and were ordered to return in a couple of weeks for arraignment. (Later, the charges were dropped when one of the airline attendants changed her testimony, saying she'd confused Morrison with Baker.)

Needless to say, they missed The Stones.

Back in Los Angeles, Morrison joined the rest of The Doors at Elektra Sound Studios. It was time for another album—the last studio album the band owed Elektra under its contract. This time, there'd be no strings and horns.

Jim: Our music has returned to the earlier form, using just four instruments. We felt we'd gone too far in the other direction (i.e., orchestration) and wanted to get back to the original, basic format.

The Doors are basically a blues-oriented group with heavy dosages of rock 'n' roll, a moderate sprinkling of jazz, a minute quantity of classical influences, and some popular elements. But basically, a white blues band.

One night, the band, along with several of their documentary crew, had dinner at Casa Escobar, a nearby Mexican restaurant, including mucho vino. Back at Elektra Studios, The Doors began a bluesy improvisational jam.

Jim: We needed another song for this album. We were racking our brains. Finally we just started playing and we played about an hour, and we went through the whole history of rock music, starting with blues, going through rock 'n' roll, surf music, Latin—the whole thing. I call it *Rock Is Dead*.

Sad to say, the jam wasn't recorded in its entirety, due to a tape change, and the interlude didn't make it onto the album. (It has since been released as part of **The Doors Box Set**.)

(previous spread) The Doors, back where they started, on the beach, for a *Morrison Hotel* photo shoot, 1969

(below) Enjoying some sanctuary at the Morrison Hotel. Downtown Los Angeles, 1970

(below) In the alcove of the Morrison
Hotel, Downtown Los Angeles, 1970

John: The music sprang from doing old stuff like "Money," or any old standard. We got that hard-rock feeling by running over all those old tunes, and then did the original tunes with the same feeling."

For the rowdy "Roadhouse Blues," a Morrison composition that signaled The Doors' determination to rock back to their roots, the band called on Lonnie Mack to play bass (as a guitarist, he'd had a big hit in 1963 with an instrumental version of Chuck Berry's "Memphis"). John Sebastian, whose band, Lovin' Spoonful, had just disbanded, played harmonica. And Ray Neopolitan, bassist on Sebastian's first solo album, served as The Doors' session bass player.

Morrison had purchased, for Pamela, a bungalow in Topanga Canyon as a more remote alternative to the apartment on Norton, near The Doors' offices. The cottage sat on a hill, not far from a juke joint, and it was that establishment that inspired "Roadhouse Blues."

Perhaps refreshed by the time off afforded him and by the scratching of so many concerts, Morrison the lyricist was back. He had a hand in the writing of every track, even if it meant digging through his poetry notebooks to find some lyrics for a soul-funk guitar riff Robby had developed.

Robby: That was "Peace Frog." I had the music for that, and Jim didn't have any words for it, so we said, "All right, let's just record it anyway." So we recorded it, and they looked through the notebook and found this cool poem. And it seemed to work. The poem, by the way, was called "Abortion Stories."

Although most of the song concerns itself with "blood in the streets," alluding to political demonstrations going on around the country, there are also lines from his poem "Awake Ghost Song," in which he tells a version of the story of his childhood vision in New Mexico.

Indians scattered on dawn's highway bleeding
Ghosts crowd the young child's fragile eggshell mind ...

Morrison Hotel, *as the album came to be called (after a successful photo shoot in a skid row hotel by that name that Manzarek had discovered), gave The Doors their fifth consecutive gold record, and*

it brought most of the music critics back onto their side. The album, Bruce Harris wrote in Jazz & Pop, "for all its flurries of autobiography, is really more directly an album about America (and) is one of the major musical events of Rock '70." But the album spawned no hits. Although it'd be a staple in their concerts, where it was a natural opening number, "Roadhouse Blues" flopped as a single.

In early 1970, with the new album out, The Doors embarked on the "Roadhouse Blues Tour." A few months after the Miami bust, they had begun picking up concert dates again, most of them promoted by their former roadie Rich Linnell and his West Coast Productions. Linnell had to post bonds with the more wary owners and managers of concert halls, guaranteeing that The Doors would not spout obscenities or incite audiences. This became known as "The Fuck Clause."

It worked, with only an occasional lapse, such as the time in Boston when Morrison muttered a ten-letter obscenity after a concert was shut down before the audience—or he—was ready to leave. The promoter of the next day's show—in Salt Lake City—canceled the concert.

But on the Roadhouse Tour, Morrison behaved. He even shaved and seemed to have slimmed down. Sometime in early 1969, he'd grown a beard, and, along with his hair and physique, it seemed to go into different states of size and health. Outside observers read his changes as attempts to renounce his sex-idol, rock-star image. His fellow Doors saw it differently.

Robby: I don't think he purposely wanted to change his image from a rock star to a drunken bum. I think that he just started eating too much and drinking too much, and he didn't look like a sex idol anymore, and it's pretty hard to be one without looking like one. I don't think it was that much of a conscious decision.

Jim Morrison looked almost preppy—clean-shaven and dressed in a dark blazer with a necktie—for his trial in Phoenix, where the airline attendant changed her testimony and set him free. But, soon after, he let himself go again.

In late March, he attended the Jim Morrison Film Festival in Vancouver staged by a pop magazine as a benefit for itself. Morrison the fledgling filmmaker, was flattered, however. His **Feast of Friends** had received mixed reviews, ranging from an award from the Atlanta Film Festival to a chorus of boos at a San Francisco screening. Now, it was being featured, along with various Doors documentaries and video shorts.

Morrison visited Vancouver again a month later, hanging out with the magazine's editor, a painter named Ihor Todoruk. He told Ihor that he'd love to go to Paris someday. Sure enough, in June, Jim had set up a trip to France and Spain. He would be accompanied by Leon Bernard.

BEWITCHED, BOTHERED, AND BEWILDERED

A funny thing happened to Jim Morrison on his way to Europe. He got married.

Well, first, he got sick. He was staying at Patricia Kennealy's apartment when he woke up with a temperature over 100 degrees. After reaching as high as 105, the fever broke, and by late afternoon, Morrison seemed to be all right, and they joined Leon for dinner.

The next night, she claimed, they really bonded. In her book, **Rock Wives**, Victoria Balfour writes:

In Patricia's eyes, the high point of her romance with Jim was when they were married in a Wiccan, or witch, ceremony in her apartment on June 24—Midsummer's Night—in 1970. Patricia, it seems, was involved with witchcraft. "It's not satanism," she is quick to say. "It's basically a mother religion, but there is also a god figure, a horned god of the hunt." Jim apparently was intrigued with all this, and it was he who suggested that they have the Wiccan wedding ceremony. So they were married by a high priest and priestess of the Celtic coven, who could have made the marriage legal, only Jim and Patricia didn't bother to get a license. "We just did the ceremony, which is binding a lot longer than till death do us part. It's a karmic sort of thing that links people through further reincarnations."

The ceremony itself involved "all kinds of rituals and candles and vows."…Patricia doesn't know how seriously Jim took the ceremony ("probably not too seriously"), but to her, going through with the

ceremony was "like being validated the way I wanted to be. It was a very private thing for me, a bond I wanted to make with this person."

Although Kennealy would ultimately write a book, **Strange Days**, that made a case for the validity of the ceremony (she even displayed a handwritten statement declaring them "wedded" and signed, in one spot, "J Morrison"), her comment to Balfour that Jim probably didn't take the event "too seriously" seemed to be more on the mark. Babe Hill, a close buddy of Morrison's, recalled asking him in Miami about the wedding. Jim told him, "I don't know what I did! I was drunk. Maybe I did, but there was no emotional involvement with her."

Morrison never told his bandmates about the ceremony.

Robby: He did mention being with a witch and stuff. But no, he never said he was married.

John: Give me a break. Pamela was Jim's soul mate. They were Romeo and Juliet and fought like hell, but they were meant to be together.

Salli Stevenson, the writer who also knew Morrison intimately, once told of playing a storytelling game of "top-this" with him. After she told her tale, Jim responded: "I got married in a witch's wedding ceremony!" When she expressed her shock, he smiled and reassured her: "Don't worry; it wasn't a real wedding; it didn't mean anything. This chick I met in New York is into witchcraft, and she was telling me about witch weddings. It seemed like a fun thing to do at the time. I was so stoned!" When Stevenson pressed him about whether or not he was "married," he responded, "Definitely not! It was joke!"

Morrison was soon off to Paris with Leon Bernard, ostensibly to do advance work for a planned tour of Europe in September. But they got little work done. Morrison had heard a lot about Paris from Alain Ronay, and this was his first chance to check it out.

He and Bernard checked into the pricey Hotel George V, and Morrison proceeded to absorb the city's sights, culture, and alcohol, visiting dozens of bars and sidewalk cafes. After a blissful week of anonymity in a beautiful city, and additional traipses through Spain and Morocco, Morrison began to feel feverish and returned home, by way of New York. But he did not visit Kennealy. Three weeks after he'd left, he

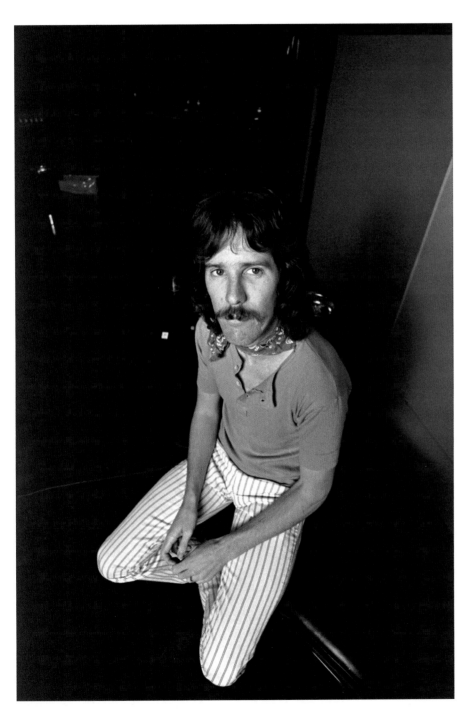

was back at the apartment on Norton Avenue, where he and Pam now lived, together and apart.

He was just in time to hear the news from Miami. The federal court there had turned down his attorney's motion to stop the trial on constitutional grounds. He responded by getting drunk.

While he was overseas, Elektra released **Absolutely Live,** *which would join all the other Doors releases to quickly become the band's sixth consecutive gold record.*

Jim: It's a fairly true document of what the band sounds like on a fairly good night. There were a few cuts that we did for the first time onstage that have flaws in them, but … in a live thing, it's just that one shot.

ON TRIAL

The State of Florida v. James Douglas Morrison, Metropolitan Dade County Justice Building, Miami, Florida, Case 69-2355.

Jim: There probably will be a big trial. I might even buy a suit. A conservative dark blue suit. And a tie. Not one of those paisley ties, but a big fat tie, with a great big knot. Maybe I'll keep a diary and publish it in *Esquire.* My impressions of my hanging.

Jim Morrison, entering the courtroom on April 10, 1970, bearded and dressed casually but nicely in a white shirt, jeans, and boots, had a case for dismissal, but he didn't have a chance. Not only was he in the South, but he had inadvertently stepped onto a political merry-go-round.

The trial judge, Murray Goodman, was up for re-election; he was appointed to fill a vacancy. Morrison's local attorney, Robert Josefsberg, had been offered the seat that Goodman took. Alfonso Sepe, the prosecutor who filed the original charges, was set to run for a seat on the bench himself.

Bill Siddons: Because there was an "acting" judge, an "acting" D.A., and an "acting" police chief—guys who were looking for political fortunes—Jim basically became a victim of the system.

(below) Jim outside the courtroom, during
his trial in Miami, 1969

*Judge Goodman shot Morrison down whenever possible. He set
sessions every other day, making if difficult for the band to work. The
jury's youngest member was forty-two years old (Jim was twenty-six).*

*The prosecution's first witness said she saw Morrison drop his pants
to his knees and touch himself. But in her statement to police in April,
she had said she didn't know whether Morrison's pants were up or
down. Her boyfriend backed up her more incriminating version,
even though, in his pretrial testimony, he said he had only a "vague
memory" of Morrison's actions. (In an article in the **Miami Herald**
in 2006, that witness, Karl Huffstutlear, stated, "I didn't see anything
come out of his drawers. To me, it's still a mystery what happened.")*

*As if he didn't have enough on his mind, Morrison got a visit, a week
into the trial, from Patricia Kennealy, who flew down from New York*

*to tell him that she was pregnant. Kennealy wrote a book about their
relationship and said that she had an abortion, but the three surviving
Doors, who traveled extensively with Morrison, say they never knew
her or of any significant relationship she may have had with Jim.*

Ray: I never knew her. I knew her as a writer and I think she was there
once to interview us, maybe once or twice at the recording studio. But
the only real image I have of her is in Miami. She was in Miami to tell Jim
she was pregnant. I didn't even know something was going on between
the two of them.

*Back in the courtroom, the defense team presented its central
argument, that The Doors' performance at the Dinner Key Auditorium
was within the bounds of the standards of the community. Besides
strippers and foul-mouth comics working the Miami Strip, there was
the rock world. Max Fink quoted Country Joe and the Fish's famous
"Fish Cheer," in which the audience spells out F-U-C-K.*

*"This is what they say and do," he argued. "A rock concert is an
expression of dissent."*

*Goodman ruled that community standards were inadmissible. An
impassioned talk by Fink about the importance of freedom of speech
also fell on deaf ears.*

Ray: He was a hanging judge. He wanted to look tough. Every time we
brought up a salient legal point concerning free speech, the rights of
the artist in contemporary American society, or community standards,
Judge Murray slammed his gavel and said, "Inadmissible evidence." We
were fucked. We had no defense except for the lack of schlong shots
and a lot of witnesses who would testify that they didn't see it, either.

*After his attorneys gained a short break in the trial, Morrison flew
off to London. Long before the trial date was set, Siddons had booked
The Doors into the Isle of Wight Festival, off the coast of England.
No matter that the band didn't like working outdoors or sharing the
bill with other superstar acts; Siddons felt they needed the business.
And so, in the middle of Morrison's trial, they gathered to play for a
Woodstock-size crowd of some six hundred thousand.*

Sharing the bill with Jimi Hendrix, Sly and the Family Stone, The Who, Ten Years After, Joni Mitchell, and others, Morrison was simply no match. He flew in directly from Miami and said he hadn't slept for thirty-six hours before hitting the stage with The Doors at around 1 A.M. "I really wasn't quite at my best."

But, unlike in his Miami concert, he actually sang songs, and well. (His performance of "When the Music's Over" is documented in the film of the festival, as is "The End," which Morrison performed between puffs on a cigarette.) He barely moved, reverting to his London Foggy routine of hanging onto the microphone as if it were some kind of support system. It turned out that—surprise!—he'd gotten drunk before going on.

John: Jim is moving nary an inch. No energy.

Ray: He sang for all he was worth but moved nary a muscle. He remained rigid and fixed to the microphone for the entire concert. Dionysus had been shackled. They had killed his spirit.

Robby: I think it was mainly the trial and all that. It really got to him. As a band, you just try to get something going, or do what you think might get Jim going. "Let's try this." That was the hard part, those nights when he wasn't into it.

Later, Morrison told reporters that the Isle of Wight was the last they'd see of him onstage.

Back in Miami, the Morrison defense team made its case, even though Judge Goodman had forced it to trim its list of witnesses to the same number the prosecution had presented. And, he ruled, there would be no "so-called experts" allowed. A parade of people swore that they hadn't seen Morrison expose himself.

On Friday, September 18, the defense rested. Judge Goodman allowed the court to be open the next day for closing statements. Saturday morning, Morrison read in the newspaper that Jimi Hendrix, who'd headlined the Isle of Wight and had followed The Doors there by a day, had died in London, an apparent drug overdose, at age twenty-seven. Earlier that month, Al Wilson, Canned Heat's guitarist, had died of an

OD, at age twenty-seven. Two weeks later, Janis Joplin would overdose in Hollywood at age twenty-seven.

Jim Morrison was still three months away from turning twenty-seven.

Closing statements took up most of Saturday, and the jury began its deliberations that evening at 9 P.M. It took them less time than the closing arguments to reach verdicts on three of the four charges. Sequestered overnight, they reconvened Sunday morning and finished their work.

It was an odd verdict. The jury found Morrison innocent of lewd behavior (a felony) but guilty of profanity (a misdemeanor). He was acquitted on the charge of public drunkenness (another misdemeanor), despite the fact that he testified that he was "too drunk" to recall whether he'd exposed himself on stage. And he was found guilty on the public exposure charge. His attorneys immediately filed an appeal, and bail, set at $50,000, was quickly posted.

As he left the courtroom, Morrison told reporters, "This trial and its outcome won't change my style, because I maintain that I did not do anything wrong."

Months later, when we spoke, he was still arguing the case. He was found not guilty of lascivious or lewd behavior, "including exposure," he noted, but guilty of indecent exposure.

Jim: So constitutionally, right there they were wrong. You're not supposed to be able to try a person on the same count twice. That's probably one of the motions that we'll include in the appeal.

In late October, he was sentenced to the max: sixty days for profanity and, for exposure, six months "at hard labor in the Dade County Jail" and a $500 fine. His lawyers expected that he might have to serve two months, plus a couple of years on probation.

When we spoke in early 1971, with his case still on appeal, he was thinking not about his own prospects—of going to jail in Florida—but about a larger picture.

Jim: You know, I was hoping—or I thought there might be a possibility of it becoming a major, groundbreaking kind of case, but it didn't turn out that way. It might have been one of the reasons why they dragged it out so long, in order not to let enough momentum or sentiment build up in a short time, or a lot of attention focus on it. So it actually received very little national attention.

I thought it might become just a basic American issue involving freedom of speech and the right of anyone with a personal viewpoint to state their ideas in public and receive a hearing without legal pressure being put on them. In fact my lawyer made a speech in which he traced the origin of freedom of speech, which goes side by side with the origin of drama, actually. It was a brilliant summary of that historical process, but it didn't have any effect on the outcome at all. The first amendment provides supposedly for the freedom of expression. There's a clause that states any dramatic or public artistic performance comes under this amendment.

Jac Holzman: Had Jim lived, he would have rejoiced that the statute on which he was arrested was later found to be unconstitutional. On appeal, his specific case would have been thrown out. And Jim would have savored with a special joy this bit of irony: The judge who tried him was himself disgraced just a few years later for taking a bribe.

In October, while Morrison awaited his sentence, he joined in a celebration. John Densmore married Julia Brose, whom he'd been seeing since early 1968, in Pacific Palisades, with Robby and his girlfriend, Lynn Veres, serving as best man and bridesmaid. Morrison, without Pam (with whom he was reportedly fighting) but with his drinking buddies, showed up, and after the bride and groom left, Jim joined the wedding band for a few numbers.

John: Jim got a little looped, but not too much, and sang and charmed the elderly. It was fun.

In 1972, the marriage ended.

(below) Jim at the original Hard Rock
Café during the *Morrison Hotel* photo
shoot. Downtown Los Angeles, 1970

(top) Ray, Lynn, Robby, and Dorothy in an open-air market enjoying pineapples, Mexico City, 1969

(bottom left) Robby at the mixing sessions for L.A. Woman.

(bottom middle) John, banging on the drums at The Doors' rehearsal space, 1970

(bottom right) Jim and Julia Brose-Densmore outside the courtroom in Miami, 1970

(right) Jim and his attorney, Max Fink, about to enter the Federal Building in Miami, 1970

11 L.A. WOMAN: BACK TO BASICS

11 L.A. WOMAN: BACK TO BASICS

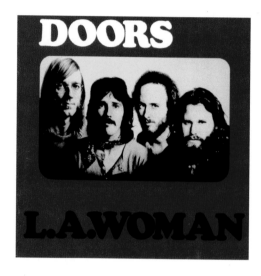

*Even before **Morrison Hotel** gave The Doors their fifth gold album, making them the first American band to have five consecutive million-copy sellers, Elektra Records went proactive to extend their relationship. The company hosted a big party for the band when they played Madison Square Garden's Felt Forum in early 1970, and Jac Holzman followed up by treating them like his own kids—kids who'd made him a millionaire. He agreed, among other things, to raise their royalty rate to 10 percent, from its original 5.*

Jac: The label made a fortune with The Doors … it was the right and proper thing for me to do.

Elektra got one more album. It turned out to be one of the best in Doors history. It began in December with—no surprise—some problems.

John: It felt good to be back at Sunset Sound, where we'd recorded our first two albums, but that was the only thing that felt good. We had been recording new songs for Paul Rothchild and there was a tense silence in the air, the same silence we encountered when Paul dropped in on our rehearsals. True, we didn't have enough songs, but Paul had a "show-me" attitude. He realized it would be another "pulling teeth" album, like *Waiting for the Sun,* which nearly killed all of us. We hadn't played the songs very well, and they weren't rehearsed enough, but I knew we had some good ones, even after all we'd been through. They were more blues-based, and the blues takes you to the root of your angst.

Paul: It was dreadful. Wall to wall boredom. Jim wasn't into it at all. He'd get into his spoiled-brat thing and drag everything down deliberately. It was the military kid showing his father what a punk he could be. It was that simple.

I worked my ass off for a week, but it was still just fucking awful. I'd go into them and tell them that, hoping that it would make them angry enough to do something good: "This isn't rock 'n' roll; it's cocktail lounge music!" But they just didn't have the heart anymore. You know, it got so bad that for the first time in my career I found myself drifting off to sleep, putting my head on the console, and nodding off.

I finally turned to Bruce Botnick and said, "I know another producer would stick with this because it's a quarter of a million dollars for the producer, but I can't do it."

I went into the studio finally and said, "Guys, I think the best thing that could happen is for me to leave, because you've become too reliant on me to come up with the energy and the ideas and the direction, and I just don't want to do it anymore. The only way you'll survive is if you make this record yourself."

John: The "fifth Door" was resigning. We were bummed. That night we were sitting in the recording studio after Rothchild had left, and Botnick could sense the gloom.

"What are we going to do, Bruce?" Ray said.

(previous spread) The Doors and Bruce Botnick during a break in the *L.A. Woman* photo shoot, 1969

(below) Goofing under the pier in Santa Monica, 1970

(left) Ray giving Robby some pointers on guitar during the *L.A. Woman* recording sessions, Los Angeles, 1970

"I'll produce you guys. We could coproduce. We could rent Wally Heider's mobile equipment and record in your rehearsal room, where you'd be real comfortable. Kind of like the old days."

He knew simplifying our recording process was the thing to do, and his suggestion sounded good.

Botnick had all the equipment brought over to 8512 Santa Monica Boulevard, and we put the recording board upstairs in Bill Siddons's office.

Bill: In fact, the console was on my desk. I would work during the day, they would come in at night, move furniture, tack blankets to the walls, and use my office as the control room.

John: We rigged a talk-back downstairs, but you couldn't see who you were talking to—no window. If you were doing overdubs it was especially eerie because you sat downstairs all alone talking to a speaker box. Everybody else was upstairs in the control room. Bruce's gentle nature created an easy atmosphere for recording, though.

Jim: We record right in our room. It's not that we don't like the Elektra studios, but we felt that we do a lot better when we're rehearsing. This will be the first record that we're actually doing without a producer. In the past, the producer—it's not that he was a bad influence or anything, but this will be a lot different without the fifth person there. So anyway, we'll be by ourselves, for better or worse.

John: Bruce's brainstorm was to let us all assume more responsibility, including Jim, and it worked. It turned out that we didn't need to control Jim in the studio. He knew the reins were slackening, and he responded by taking more responsibility. Bruce never pushed us beyond a couple of takes; the vocals didn't have to be pulled out of Jim because most of them were live. We couldn't have gotten to this place without doing several albums with Rothchild.

Sixteen-track recording had been invented, and in fact we'd used it on the album before, but Botnick suggested that we record *L.A. Woman* on portable eight-track machines.

Bill Siddons: *L.A. Woman* was a very visceral record. They intentionally made it closer to the bone. They had been high-teched out with *The Soft Parade* and "Take 35." Their last record turned out like their first album: raw and simple. It was as if they had come full circle. Once again they were a garage band.

Jim: The first album we did in about ten days, and then each succeeding record took longer and longer until the last one (*Morrison Hotel*), which took nine months. This one, we went in and got a song a day. It was amazing, partly because we went back to the original instrumentation: just the four of us and a bass player. We're using Elvis's bass player...

That was Jerry Scheff. In addition, for rhythm guitar, The Doors brought in Marc Benno, a Texas blues guitarist who would go on to work with Leon Russell, Eric Clapton, and Lightnin' Hopkins.

John: We never fought while making records. People have said, "Well, in his last years, Jim was going down..." But even *L.A. Woman:* he somehow managed. When the doors were closed and the public was not privy to our rehearsing, we were back in the garage, back to the purity of the four of us. We could make magic, no matter how fucked up he was. Somehow we did the whole album in two weeks. We get together and we're teenagers in the garage again, because Jim did care about what we were doing, and we pulled it off.

Robby: I'd say by *Morrison Hotel,* we'd run out of songs, so we pretty much were doing it at the studio as we went along. "Riders on the Storm" we were just playing "Ghost Riders in the Sky" one day for fun, and Jim came up with "Ghost Riders on the Storm, Ghost Riders in the Sky."

"Riders on the Storm" and "L.A. Woman" were two quintessential Doors-type songs that just kind of came together magically in the studio. "L.A. Woman," I think we just did that in the studio one day, just playing it.

Actually, "L.A. Woman," the title track, came from a poem Jim Morrison wrote about his love/hate relationship with his city. Or was it? Michael Ford, a poet and radio commentator, was a longtime friend of Morrison's.

(right) A poem Jim gave to Diane Gardiner, written on her own stationery, 1970

Michael: A poet doesn't just hand his work over to people. Diane Gardiner was a recipient of a bulk of his work. "L.A. Woman" is Los Angeles, but Diane Gardiner was a magnet for the concept of "L.A. Woman."

I always felt, when Jim talked about it, that she was an undisclosed impetus for his writing that tune. It was more ethereal than anything. She wasn't a star-chaser. She seemed to be someone Jim appreciated a lot more than the others.

Diane: Somewhere stashed away, I've got some stuff that he wrote for me, or that appeared to be written for me, and that appeared in the last album. Who knows? Maybe he went to everybody's house and did that, just to make them feel good!

On one sheet of a notepad Diane used at Rogers, Cowan & Brenner, Jim scribbled:

I just got her(e) about an hour ago
Looking around to see which way the winds blows
Where the little girls in the Hollywood Bungalows…

Those lines would, with a few changes, be part of "L.A. Woman." Gardiner said that Morrison often wrote and did drawings at her apartment, downstairs from the one Jim had rented for Pamela and, sometimes, himself.

Motel money
Murder madness
Let's change the mood
From glad to sadness…

Diane: It's things that happened. "Into your blues, into your blue, blue, blues." I was always playing him blues in my apartment. "L.A. Woman" was like a description of exactly what happened to us.

"Us?" Was the publicist and her client in a relationship? Yes, she said. And, somehow, she managed to remain friends with Pamela.

Diane: When "L.A. Woman" came out, she said, "Well, at least I got the line *I see your hair is burning*," she said. "That's all I get."

On December 8, Morrison celebrated his twenty-seventh birthday by taking his poetry notebooks and a few friends into a studio in Los Angeles, Village Recorders. He wanted to record some new poetry and rerecord some of the material he'd put down before with engineer John Haeny—who was, once again, at the controls. The friends, some of whom joined in on the readings, included Frank Lisciandro and his wife, Kathy, who was a secretary for The Doors, Alain Ronay, his friend from UCLA, and a friend of his, Florentine Pabst.

The session would go on for four hours, until a drunken Morrison could barely stand.

THE BATTLE OF NEW ORLEANS

Although Morrison had said he'd done his last concert at the Isle of Wight, The Doors worked a couple of cities in December. In Dallas, on the eleventh, they did what everyone agreed was a successful show. The next day, they found themselves at the Warehouse in New Orleans. For whatever reason, Morrison imploded.

Ray: Everyone who was there saw it, man. He lost all his energy about midway through the set. He hung on the microphone and it just slipped away. You could actually see it leave him. He was drained. Jim picked up the microphone stand and repeatedly bashed it into the stage, over and over until there was the sound of wood splintering. He threw the stand into the stunned audience, turned, and plopped down on the drum riser, sitting motionless.

John: Yeah, that was pathetic. It was a gig where we only got through about half the set. It was just completely lame. Everything caught up with him. He was tired. There was no passion. He started telling stupid jokes. It was really sad. It was the end of our live career, and I was pleased. What we created was so special to me; it was so magical, and it was being eroded. I hated it.

Although it's been said that, at one point, Morrison planted himself on Densmore's drum riser, and Densmore planted a boot on his back and kicked him off, John disputes that story, and tells one of his own.

John: He was sitting on my riser and would not get up. And I got up and sat down next to him. Ray and Robby kept vamping. I go, "What

Memo from: Date:

DIANE GARDINER

So I took a room in the
heart of town
Got wound & the wife
came round
Said 3 yrs have now
gone by
What's the plan, what's
the action

Arrival visit transcent
drawl
That's all
I said "That is all."

ROGERS, COWAN & BRENNER, INC.

song do you want to do, Jim? We're in front of thousands of people. Let's
do something."

*Back in Los Angeles, The Doors began 1971 by wrapping up L.A.
Woman. Morrison was pleased about the homey, blues-drenched
sessions, with songs ranging from John Lee Hooker's "Crawling
King Snake" to a poem he'd written in 1968, "Texas Radio," that he'd
recited in concerts. Now, it was extended into a song, "The Wasp
(Texas Radio & the Big Beat)." But while he sang about a musical
rhythm he used to hear, as a kid, on border radio, he was also talking
about escape.*

The Negroes in the forest
brightly feathered
And they are saying
"Forget the night! Live with us in
forests of azure
Out here on the perimeter, there are
no stars
Out here we is stoned—immaculate"

THINKING ABOUT PARIS

*One afternoon in February, I was hanging out with Diane Gardiner in
her apartment on Norton Avenue. With us was Earl McGrath, a record
producer, screenwriter, and friend to The Rolling Stones.*

*There was a rap on the door. It was Jim Morrison, and he was looking
for Pam. She wasn't home, Diane said, and invited Jim to stick around
and wait for her. Diane liked gathering friends at her place.*

*I hadn't met Morrison before—Jerry Hopkins had done most of our
coverage of the band, and I didn't know much about what was going
on with The Doors, aside from some gossip that he was heading off
to France. With his full beard and the beginnings of a beer belly, he
didn't look much like the rock star of old. I wasted no time asking
for an interview. He hadn't said much in the aftermath of the verdict
in Miami, and, on the eve of his departure to Europe, I thought he
might be willing to comment on the state of Jim Morrison and of*

11 L.A. WOMAN: BACK TO BASICS

The Doors. Sure, he said. He had nothing better to do. I grabbed my cassette recorder.

And then things got weird. Jim got playful, and suggested that we pretend as though we were doing a talk show on TV—he specifically mentioned **The Dick Cavett Show,** *and we arranged two chairs to face each other at a forty-five-degree angle. He then sat down and told a joke, one he'd apparently used on stage. "What's the difference between an intelligent midget and a female track star?" he asked. I shrugged. "Well, one of them is a cunning runt!"*

But, soon, we settled into a pretty serious conversation. He got into it enough that when Pamela showed up, he continued with our chat. And she joined in, too. Here are a few excerpts from what turned out to be his last interview.

How much longer do you have with Elektra?

Well, we're at work on our last album for them.

Do you see far beyond that?

I can't see too much beyond that. You know, it's a day-to-day thing. I think with this album we're at kind of a crossroads in our career. So, we'll know within the next five or six months what the future will be.

What's in the immediate future? Any concerts?

No, we're kind of off playing concerts; somehow no one enjoys the big places anymore, and to go into clubs more than just a night every now and then is meaningless.

A few years ago, we were probably right on for the age of people who would go to large concerts, whereas now we may appeal to an older audience, maybe still the Fillmore crowds. But I would say it would be an anachronism for the younger people.

Do you think you'd be classified among the people who signify what some people insist is the "death of rock?"

Well, I was saying rock is dead years ago. Twenty or thirty years ago, jazz was the kind of music people went to, and large crowds danced to, and moved around to. And then rock 'n' roll replaced that, and then another generation came along and they called it rock. The new generation of kids will come along in a few years, swarm together, and have a new name for it. It'll be the kind of music that people like to go out and get it on to.

Each generation wants new symbols, new people, and new names. They want to divorce themselves from the preceding generation, and so they won't call it rock, they'll invent some new name for it.

(About fifteen minutes into our visit, Pamela arrives, along with her dog, Sage, and Jim asks whether or not she has any wine or beer. He then gets onto the phone to order delivery of some staples, including potato chips and a half-pint of Beefeater gin. Diane, Pamela, and I chat while he places the order.)

Why have you gotten fat, Jim? That was the question we were discussing.

Pamela: Who says he's fat? I like it!

Jim: I guess it's just a natural aging process…Maybe it's not being as physically active. I think it's mainly just filling out. Some people have that kind of build.

Does touring and running around doing that kind of thing make you lose a lot of weight?

Jim: I would say if you performed a lot and sweated a lot and moved around.

Pam: It's mainly drinking.

Jim: I drink a lot of beer. While I'm recording, especially. If you drink hard liquor when you're recording pretty soon you're so out of it, you can't do anything anymore. But beer—it gives you a little energy and you can keep going all night. Beer puts on the pounds.

What did you do in Miami during your spare time? Weren't you sort of captive in the city?

Jim: Yeah, sometimes it would be two days, sometimes three days a week. I had a chance to do a little waterskiing. I learned how to scuba dive. I went to Nassau for a weekend. They have beautiful underwater natural parks. Have you ever scuba dived? It's a beautiful trip. You're just floating. It's an intrauterine experience.

One thing I was interested to observe: Every day we would rush home to watch ourselves on TV; they couldn't film in the courtroom, but going and leaving they'd film it, and we'd hear the reporters' views of what happened. The first few days it was kinda the old-line policy, what people had been thinking for a year and a half, but as the trial wore on, the reporters themselves, from just talking to me and the people involved in the case—the tone of the news articles—and even the papers—became a little more objective as each day went on.

[Later, the talk turned to The Beatles. Jim had been reading **Rolling Stone** *editor Jann Wenner's two-part interview with John Lennon.]*

Jim: In a way, we came along at a weird time, at the tail end of the rock revival from England. You know, they'd already done it. I think it was the success of those English groups that gave hope to a lot of musicians over here, saying, "Sheee-it, we can do the same thing!"

[Morrison put forth the proposition that, just as movie stars and rock stars had been heroes to society, so an activist journalist could fill that role in the future. I asked whether a poet might be a hero.]

Jim: Poets usually become heroes after they're long gone, and with writers, it's with an intellectual crowd. But, I mean, everyone reads newspapers and magazines, even if they just skim through them. I do that with the *Rolling Stone* and the *Free Press* and other things.

Pam: I like the idea of a journalist that could become a hero.

Jim: Not a journalist, I don't think, I think a journalist/editor, a publisher, you know, publishing his own magazine…Like Dickens used to edit a newspaper. *Oliver Twist, Scrooge,* he wrote all those things, and he edited a magazine when he was at the height of his fame; he was read by everyone in England.

Pam: They had more time to read in those days.

Jim: Well, they didn't have TV.

Pam: When they came home, they'd sit down and read it out loud to everybody.

Jim: That was their records and TV and movies, all wrapped into one.

Jim Morrison had begun thinking about going to Paris since December, when Pamela returned from France. She wanted to move there, she told Jim, with or without him. But she'd prefer him to be there, to be away from Los Angeles, to write, to get healthier.

Pamela left for Paris on Valentine's Day, to find an apartment for the two of them. But it wasn't until early March, at a mixing session for **L.A. Woman,** *that he told The Doors that he was leaving. He said he needed a break, and that he wasn't sure how long he'd be gone. He then left the studios.*

Until that point, says Diane Gardiner, he hadn't made a firm decision.

Diane: Pamela would send him postcards saying, "I'm fine except I cry all the time because I miss you." It was a very up and down thing; it was a "should I or should I not," and maybe we're all delusional; maybe all women who had any contact with Jim are nuts, but I believe that I could have said "Stay" and he would have stayed. Instead I moved to Sausalito (in Marin County, north of San Francisco) to work with Jefferson Airplane and said, "Why don't you move on to Paris?" And he did.

As he began to make his farewells, Morrison gave different friends different impressions of his mental state. One remembered him playing touch football with energy and enthusiasm. Another thought that "the dark side was taking over," and that he was still drinking heavily. And John Haeny, who'd recorded Jim's poetry on his birthday, said he got a call from Morrison, who told him he was going away "to work on his reading voice. To clarify his poetic thoughts and to organize his words and ideas."

Morrison's drinking buddy, Tom Baker, he of that flight that got them busted in Phoenix, showed up in Los Angeles just before Jim left. They hadn't seen each other since a drunken fight eight months before.

Tom Baker: We went to an outdoor restaurant and reaffirmed our friendship. He told me he'd had the opportunity to patch things up with our old drinking buddy Janis Joplin ... Apparently he made amends with her just weeks before she passed away, and he was genuinely grateful for it. Jim was drinking, although he was restricting himself to white wine. I looked at him and remembered the first time I had seen him. His once sharply defined face was now bloated by alcohol; his features were soft and pale. His eyes lacked that fierce sparkle and he moved with what appeared to be great effort ... He confided to me his intention to move to Paris. "Yeah," he said, "my rock 'n' roll days are over, I guess."

Along with Babe Hill we would meet quite regularly for the rest of his time in L.A. and I could tell he had lost much of his fascination for that town. His last day in L.A., he and Babe and I spent wandering around the Santa Monica pier. Late in the afternoon, we returned to his office and he tossed notebooks, manuscripts, and other belongings into cardboard boxes. Various friends stopped by to wish him bon voyage. In the morning he boarded his flight.

12 FREE MAN IN PARIS

12 FREE MAN IN PARIS

End w/ fond good-bye...
Which of my cellves
Will be remembered
Good-bye America
I loved you
—Road Days / Wilderness

"My rock 'n' roll days are over," Jim Morrison declared to Tom Baker just before taking off for Paris.

Bill Siddons: Jim moved to Paris to find out who he was creatively. He had left the band. He had felt controlled and manipulated by the band for quite a while, and there was a lot of animosity there, although no hostility. So he went to find a different muse.

And yet, when we spoke, just before he departed, Morrison said, "I think we'll do a couple more albums, then everyone will probably get into their own things. I think each guy in the band has projects that they want to do more independently. I think that Robby would like to do a predominately guitar thing. And John likes jazz, and I would suspect he might produce and play on a jazz album of his own."

But in L.A., the three Doors weren't thinking about doing projects on their own. They were still planning on working as The Doors, and, according to Manzarek, had no thought that Jim might not return, or might want to do something else.

Ray: Robby and I and John are working on songs, getting together and rehearsing two times a week. Jim never told any of us about wanting to quit. Jim not play music, not sing? I couldn't imagine it.

John: I knew we were going to keep playing music. We didn't know what we were going to do, and we didn't know what he was going to do.

In mid-June, John got a call from Jim in Paris. According to John, Jim asked how *L.A. Woman* was doing.

"Great!" Densmore responded. "'Love Her Madly' is a hit and everyone really likes the album."

"Well," said Morrison, "maybe we should do another one."

"When do you think you might come back?" Densmore asked.

"Oh, a few months."

John: But I knew we were going on without him. And I was relieved. I just hoped Ray and Robby would go for it. He can't come back, I thought. He would just want to play the blues, the slow, soulful, monotonous

(below) Jim at a sidewalk café in Paris,
weeks before his death, 1971

(below) "The Bandit Up in the Hills" – at a
café in Paris, 1971

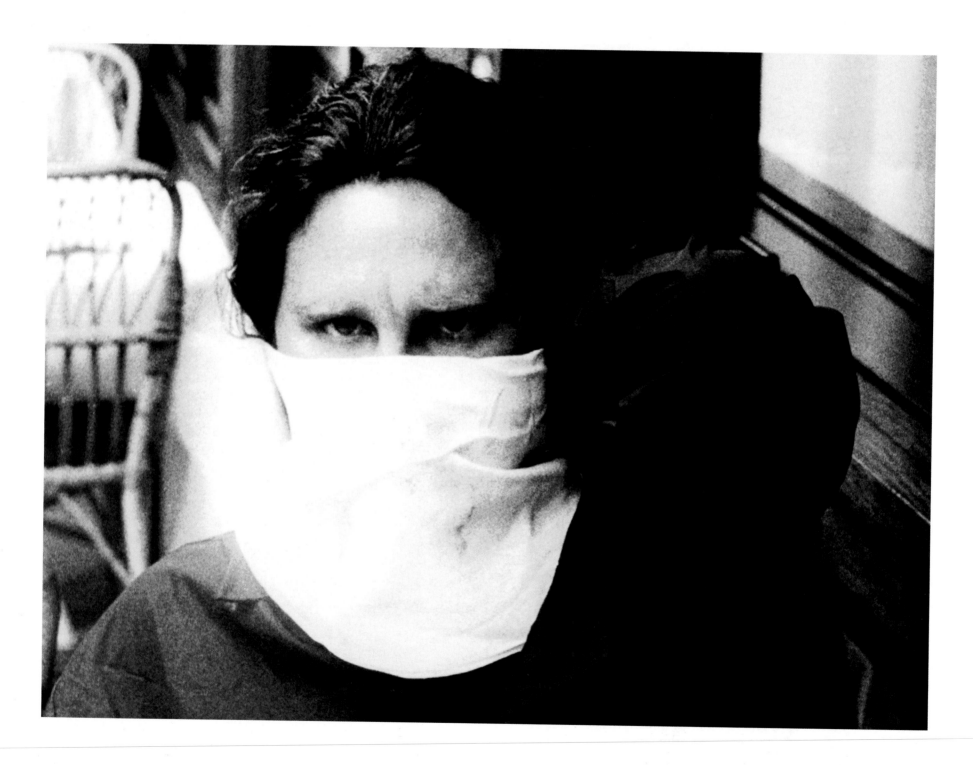

blues, which is great for a singer like him, but boring for a drummer like me. If he came back I knew the other band members would give in. Even I wouldn't be able to say no.

They said good-bye, and Densmore remembered sighing and thinking to himself, "Wait till I tell the others. They won't believe he wants to make another record ..."

Whatever he told the others, Manzarek says he thought Densmore told Morrison that they were waiting for his return, and even talking about touring again. But, given Densmore's feelings about working with Morrison, and the band's decision to stop touring after the New Orleans disaster, it's unlikely that Densmore would have made such a suggestion. Unless, of course, a changed and recharged Jim Morrison came back from Paris.

Ray: We were waiting for Jim to come back and we'd go on the road and tour *L.A. Woman* just the way we did it in the recording studio. It would have been a motherfucker, man!

I was expecting him to come back as the poet reborn. I thought the time in Paris would be great for his writing. And he could get away from his "drinking buddies," refresh himself.

In hindsight, that was wishful thinking. In May, in Paris, Jim was talking with a couple of new friends, Hervé Muller, a writer for a rock magazine, *Rock et Folk*, and his girlfriend, Yvonne Fuka, the magazine's art director. Muller expressed interest in producing French translations of *Feast of Friends* and *HWY*. Morrison had taken copies of various Doors-related films and videos for a possible screening in France. As they talked over a couple of bottles of wine, Jim told Yvonne essentially what he'd told Tom Baker.

Jim: I'm twenty-seven years old. That is too old to be a rock singer. It doesn't make sense anymore. I'm so sick of everything. People keep thinking of me as a rock 'n' roll star and I don't want anything to do with it. I can't stand it anymore. I'd be so glad if people didn't recognize me ...

Depending on who saw and hung out with him in Paris, or who got

Enjoying Paris or hating it: Patricia Kennealy, who says she received several letters from Jim (but did not reproduce any in her book), but Tere Tereba, who'd been a model in the magazine shoot about Pamela's boutique, ran into the couple and wrote to a friend at *Crawdaddy!* magazine: "Jim proceeds to tell me how he loves Paris, even though neither he nor Pamela can speak French." In a letter in late June, just days before his death, he told his accountant, Bob Greene, "The weather finally turned sunny today after a month of gray, Paris is beautiful in the sun, an exciting town, built for human beings."

Well or ill: Jim was still recovering from a spill he'd taken in Los Angeles early in the year, and had picked up a viral infection, which triggered his asthma, which he had since childhood. He was constantly coughing—and smoking. But he also lost weight, shaved his beard, and appeared healthy to friends and acquaintances—healthy enough, anyway, to take trips with Pamela to Morocco and Corsica.

Drinking or not: Alain Ronay, his French friend from UCLA days, saw Morrison in May, and noted that "he wasn't drinking very much." But people he met in town, including Hervé Muller and his friend Gilles Yepremian, told stories about Morrison drinking himself senseless one night, and, the next morning, drinking Bloody Marys while waiting for lunch, and then skipping his meal, instead drinking scotch and cognac.

Productive or not: "He wrote practically every day," said Ronay. Tere Tereba recalled Jim showing her some of his recent writings, and said he hoped to publish a handwritten book. But others say he sometimes sat for hours and produced only bits and pieces. He wrote "As I Look Back," which would be published in the posthumous collection called *Wilderness*:

Venice Summer
Drug Visions
Roof top songs
early struggles & humiliations
Thanks to the girls
who fed me

Optimistic about his projects or not: Although he had not been able to complete his poetry album while in the United States, he told Tereba that he'd received offers for stage and screen work, but preferred to concentrate on his writing.

Thinking long-term or sensing an end in sight: In his letter to his accountant, he inquired about having enough funds for him and Pam to stay in Paris for "the indefinite future." But Kennealy wrote that in a letter to her in June, "he speaks of standing on the downslope to a void," and that "he writes that he thinks he wants to be dead ..." And, in June, he visited Père Lachaise Cemetery, the final resting place for such artists as Edith Piaf, Frederic Chopin, Gertrude Stein, Marcel Proust, and Oscar Wilde. He told a friend that he would like to be buried there someday.

Alain: One night we had a conversation that was totally moving. It was full of affection ... Jim telling funny stories about his dad and so on. The stories were really tender and warm. I wish his parents could've heard it. I really felt that he'd totally reclaimed himself.

Morrison knew that his mother had expressed concern about his health just before he left for Paris. His parents were in Washington, D.C., and Jim reportedly asked Pamela to call them, to assure them that he was taking care of himself.

Anne: Had Jim had the time to live on, I think there would've been a reconciliation; I have no doubt he had some admiration for them.

(below) Having fun with the camera,
Paris, 1971

THE DEATH OF JAMES DOUGLAS MORRISON

A few months before Paris, Jim sat for an interview with his friend from Circus magazine, Salli Stevenson. With her were two other Circus staffers, one of whom, to Salli's horror, asked Jim, "How do you think you'll die?"

Jim: I hope at about the age of 120 with a sense of humor and a nice comfortable bed. I wouldn't want anybody around. I'd just want to quietly drift off.

He may have gotten his wish. In the early morning hours of Saturday, July 3, Jim Morrison died in the apartment he and Pamela were subletting. (Soon after his arrival, they settled into a spacious apartment at 17 rue Beautreillis, on the Right Bank, in the Marais arrondissement.)

From the moment that Pamela discovered him unconscious in the bathtub, his death has been shrouded in mystery.

Although rumors circulated around Paris, no one in America knew anything until Bill Siddons issued a statement on July 9, a statement crafted by Bob Hilburn, the Los Angeles Times' chief pop music critic.

"I have just returned from Paris where I attended the funeral of Jim Morrison," he began. "Jim was buried in a simple ceremony, with only a few close friends present. The initial news of his death and funeral was kept quiet because those of us who knew him intimately and loved him as a person wanted to avoid all the notoriety and circuslike atmosphere that surrounded the deaths of Janis Joplin and Jimi Hendrix.

"I can say that Jim died peacefully of natural causes," Siddons continued. ("The official cause was heart failure.) "He had been in Paris since March with his wife, Pam. He had seen a doctor in Paris about a respiratory problem and had complained of his problem on Saturday—the day of his death."

For my obituary in Rolling Stone, I called Siddons. "There was no service, and that made it all the better," he said. "We just threw some flowers and dirt and said good-bye," said Siddons. I had learned that there had been no autopsy. *Why not? "Just because we didn't want to do it that way. We wanted to leave him alone. He died in peace and dignity."*

Still, as I reported in Rolling Stone:

Someone botched things up. Rumors leaked out from Paris to London that weekend that Morrison had died. But when reporters called Jim and Pam's flat, near the Bastille, they reported being told that Morrison was "not dead but very tired and resting in a hospital."

As late as July 8, after he had been buried, United Press International's Paris office was reporting Morrison "recovering and being treated in a hospital or sanitarium." A pop paper in Paris ran a photo of Morrison with the headline reading "Jim Morrison Not Dead," reporting him "tired" from "a minor malady."

His death was kept absolutely secret. Saturday night, however, a disc jockey in a local nightclub reported the death over the loudspeaker. His announcement was greeted with surprise and silence. A small current of talk spread, landed in London that night, and reverberated back to Paris for comment and details. There were none.

The American Embassy didn't hear rumors until Monday. Finally, Pam Morrison filed the death certificate on Wednesday, listing Jim as James Morrison, poet. The embassy didn't realize until Friday, when news agencies began pressing for the story, that the dead man was Jim Morrison of The Doors.

None of the other Doors believed the news—perhaps because they'd heard it so many times before—until Siddons personally told them.

John: I was in the office, and Robby was there. It was a combination of shock—because I thought that maybe he's gonna be an Irish drunk living to eighty—and relief for his spirit. He was pretty tortured, you know.

Robby: It was disbelief. We would hear stuff like that every once in a while about Jim—"Oh, he fell out a third floor window, he's dead"—so I didn't really believe it, until Bill Siddons went over there and said it was true. And then after that, what are you going to do? He's gone. It was terrible, the worst thing that could have happened. But not unexpected, although in a way, I thought, he'll be around forever, he'll outlive all of us.

Ray: It was just a tragic loss. That was a poet, an artist who had many more great works within him. That was my greatest loss: that he was not going to be able to give the world his observations on the world and on the interior human being. He was not going to be able to share with us his life, his love for being alive, and his madness and his wildness and his darkness and his love at the same time.

The main point was the loss of the artist, and then the loss of a friend. My buddy is gone. It was like, "Wow, this can't be over. We've got way too much to do; this can't be over."

For Jim's parents, who had not had contact with him since before he formed The Doors, the news was obviously a shock.

Adm. Morrison: It's not something you can really describe. We were notified by the Naval attaché ... the embassy in Paris sent me a message and said that Jim had died of a heart attack. He had the information on a death certificate and he would send it to us. That was the shock we got.

Andy: I was shooting pool and my brother-in-law called up and told me to come home. They'd heard it on the radio. The Doors people didn't notify my parents.

Anne: A friend called and told my husband. He said, "It's on the radio that he's died." It was days later when we heard it. Jim was already buried.

The way I looked at it, he's gone and that's too bad and I knew his lifestyle, so it wasn't any big surprise.

Losing him was awful. It took me a long, long time to get over it. My brother was here, but my parents were somewhere else. It was hard because of all the speculation that maybe he wasn't dead. You had that little bit of "maybe."

The Morrison family had no problem with Père Lachaise being his final resting place.

Adm. Morrison: I was impressed with the fact that here was my son getting into a great cemetery in Paris. I thought it was quite an honor for him and the family to have a man in that position where he's side-by-side with the great literary people of the past century.

And obviously there was attention being paid by hundreds and hundreds of people that kept coming there ... it was very impressive to realize how known and liked he was.

I was impressed with the tomb and the attention it was given. We were concerned about graffiti and so on, and we had several meetings with cemetery officials and they were very cooperative.

The family has provided funds to Père Lachaise to assure that the gravesite is guarded and kept clean, along with the surrounding area. In 1990, the Morrisons placed a permanent granite headstone on the grave, with a bronze plaque.

Anne: My dad thought for a long time about what to put on the grave. He reads ancient Greek, so he put, in Greek, "True to His Own Spirit."

The inscription, KATA TON DAIMONA EAYTOY, translates literally to: "To the divine spirit within himself."

Anne: Jim was a gentleman; he was very gracious, and he was very funny. What I would like to know is what he might have been.

Mom kept a whole scrapbook; there's a whole envelope of clippings. She was proud of him. It took Dad a while to come around, with kind of the moral issues. He's a very moral guy; mom's a little more lenient on that. She was proud to send stuff off to the Rock and Roll Hall of Fame when they asked for it.

C.A.P. No 52898
JIM
AMERICAN
PRAYER
MORRISON
MERCI POUR
NOUS AVOIR
ELEVER
ZOEUF
1943 - 1971

AT 17 RUE BEAUTREILLIS

Nobody bought the official version of the story of how Jim Morrison died. His heart just stopping at age twenty-seven? No autopsy? Bill Siddons never looked into the coffin to confirm that Morrison was dead? A sealed coffin put into the ground in Paris? A six-day delay between his death and an announcement to the media?

In Rolling Stone, *I relayed what, in those early days of July, 1971, comprised the official version of events.*

It is known that Morrison had a respiratory ailment and had been coughing up blood for nearly two months in Paris. He saw two doctors during that time, but up to the time of his death, appeared strong and healthy.

Around 4 A.M. Saturday, July 3, Morrison woke up, disturbed. He was coughing again, and when he awoke, he threw up a small quantity of blood. But, Siddons said, Jim told Pam he felt OK and that he wanted to take a bath.

Pamela, twenty-five, apparently went back to sleep. Then she decided to check on him. "Jim was dead in the bathtub," said Siddons. "He had a half-smile on his face, and at first Pamela thought he was kidding, putting her on. But he was dead." Pam called the fire department to attempt resuscitation, and the police and a doctor followed—all too late.

The death certificate listed the cause of death as a heart attack. Some early news reports said a sudden case of pneumonia led to the death. Siddons said he knew the exact cause of death but couldn't describe it in official medical terms. "It was some sort of heart failure," he said, complicated by a possible lung infection. "Blood probably collected from a clot and worked its way up the chest and blocked heart valves. And that caused the heart attack."

Siddons attributed the blood clot to "physical abuse."

Just how Jim Morrison died is one of the classic rock 'n' roll mysteries. We cannot solve the case here. Entire books have been devoted to the numerous scenarios and theories, many of them involving hard drugs, that have surfaced since that morning in Paris.

Penny Courson, a well-read woman, has heard the roll call of rumors, about Morrison ODing on heroin, which he mistook for cocaine. "They say he snorted China White or American red, white, or blue, or whatever color it was." About the drugs having been provided by Pamela's friend, Count Jean de Breteuil. About the Count (whose name came up as the source of the heroin that killed Janis Joplin the previous October, and who himself would soon die of a heroin OD) coming to their apartment early in the morning, needing to break through a locked bathroom door, and helping her to concoct a story for the police.

Penny Courson: What I believe happened—what Pamela told us—was that they had been out, and they had been to a movie that wasn't very good, and they ate some food—some sweet-and-sour cooking—and got home. Jim had been coughing and coughing the whole time in Paris. There was no sunshine; it was dark and gloomy, and he needed to get into some sun. That's when they went on their trip to Spain.

And she said that they were exhausted; he was playing some music and also writing some poetry, and they finally went to bed. He was still coughing, and finally she said, "You've got to soak in the tub," because he was an asthmatic. So she drew a hot tub, for the steam. Pamela says she got back into bed and fell asleep. And when she awakened, he wasn't there. She went into the bathroom and found him in the tub. There was no mention of the door being locked—none of that.

At first she thought he was teasing; it looked like he had a smile and then she told me, she started yelling, "Jim, don't! You're scaring me!"

Imagine being three thousand miles away from home and trying to use the phone and knowing no French…and, so…I don't know that she called de Bruteuil, because he was in town, he would be able to help as far as who to call and how to call and so forth; she then called the fire department and the police.

Ms. Courson doesn't buy the stories about Morrison overdosing. "I have no idea," she said, "and I don't believe Jim would have used heroin; I don't think he would have approved of Pam doing it." Told that Morrison was known to have disapproved of Pam's use of heroin, her mother nodded. "Right," she said, in a hushed tone. Still, she didn't think Morrison died because of drugs.

Penny Courson: It's my feeling, from what I know about medicine, which is considerable—later in life, I worked in a laboratory owned by a great pathologist—I think what happened is that Jim suffered a blood clot to the lung, and that was it.

That morning, in her distress, Pamela called Alain Ronay and his friend, the filmmaker Agnès Varda. They rushed to the apartment and helped her to call and to deal with the authorities. They also helped to get a plot at Père Lachaise for Jim's body.

"In peace and dignity."

Was it an accident? What, then, to make of a note from Jim, set against a lamp in the apartment? It read:

Last Words, Last Words, Out.

Bill Siddons: There's all kinds of theories, but it goes along with why I didn't look at the body. I loved and honored Jim too much to want to see him dead. And I love and honor him too much to want to deal with all these scurrilous rumors. I always believed Jim died of a heart attack. And if something else happened, something else happened.

And, finally, as for the truth of his identification of Pam as Morrison's wife in that statement to the press...

Bill: Pam showed me a marriage certificate when I was in Paris with her. It may have been a gesture on my part. Clearly no one else in Jim's life was ever as close to him as she was. The detail as to whether or not it was filed with the local government—of *course* she was his wife. She was his soul wife, if nothing else.

(**left**) *Other Voices*, Topanga, CA, 1972

OTHER VOICES: THE DOORS CARRY ON

John: Robby said we should have let there be a space, a mourning period, before we continued.

Robby: I don't know how long we waited before we decided to go on. But at one point we had to decide what we were going to do. We had been rehearsing while Jim was gone, we had some new songs that I had written, and I said, "What the hell, let's do it ourselves."

The Doors did their best, and that was pretty good, as they'd shown at various concerts, from the Whisky a Go Go to Amsterdam, when they had to fill in for Jim Morrison.

But, as vital as they were to the music of The Doors, for Manzarek, Krieger, and Densmore to go on without their front man was just not going to work. The four sides of The Doors diamond had been reduced to three.

At Elektra Records, Jac Holzman realized this. But, although he had no further legal claims to The Doors, he generously offered the surviving members a recording contract for five albums, and the three musicians produced two: **Other Voices** *and* **Full Circle,** *with Manzarek and Krieger being those other voices, and with all three sharing songwriting duties and credits.*

John: It was to pay back for our success. We had the sense not to try and replace Jim. We didn't want to fall into the trap of having somebody trying to fill his shoes—or his leather pants. Ray and Robby tried to sing, and we did two albums and quit, and that was good, because it wasn't the magic without Jim.

Robby: I thought it was nice of Jac Holzman to sign us again. He didn't have to. I think those albums sold well enough that he could recoup pretty much anyway. We certainly could have gone on and done a third one, but we just couldn't get along anymore after Jim was gone. The three of us had always gotten along fine before that, but once that one cog is gone out of the wheel, then the balance is not there anymore, so we couldn't do it.

Once Jim was gone, each of our little egos started to take over and we couldn't get along anymore musically.

Ray: We did *Other Voices* and then we did *Full Circle.* The music was good. Two thirds of those songs were excellent songs, and it became a matter of "I don't like Ray's voice; I don't like Robby's voice. I'm sorry, Jim was better than you." OK, well, if Jim was singing those songs, "Tightrope Ride" would've been a mother. If Jim had been singing John's song "Ships with Sails," holy cow. There's a whole bunch of stuff that, had Jim been around to sing, they would be considered first-rate songs.

"Tightrope Ride," sung by Ray in a rocking, Rolling Stones voice, offered words of advice—too little, too late—aimed directly at Jim:

Don't go over the line
You better keep on time
Or you'll lose your mind
On your tightrope ride

Issued as a single, "Tightrope Ride" peaked at No. 71 in the **Billboard** *charts early in 1972. The Doors continued to tour, playing smaller venues but drawing good notices.*

Ray: Then we thought, "It's time to get a lead singer." In 1973, we went to London. The possibilities were Joe Cocker—what a great singer! Howard Werth, of a band called Audience. We talked about a lot of people. Iggy Pop was brought up, and I said, "Hey! Paul McCartney, he sings and plays bass!" I wouldn't have to play bass anymore if we had Paul McCartney! We could've supplied the John Lennon darkness to Paul McCartney's lightness, and something very interesting could have happened. But none of that came to fruition as we were rehearsing.

Robby: Going to London was probably a stupid idea, because it was so cold that they had blackouts, and at night the hotels turned the heat off, so you're fucking freezing, and it was raining all the time—it was just depressing. And Dorothy was pregnant and she was going crazy, and Ray decided to go home. That was when we broke up.

(below) Pam and Jim together at the
Bronson Caves in the Hollywood Hills,
1970

Ray: Working on the new songs, the thought occurred to me: jazz rock. This is our new direction; it's gonna be like "Riders on the Storm," let's go with that stuff! I told John and Robby, and a day or two later, John said to me, "We talked about it and we decided it should be hard rock, not jazz rock." And I said, "Huh? You've decided? Who's 'we'? You two? OK." The next day I said, "I've decided something also: I quit. Dorothy and I are going home." I didn't want to play hard rock anymore. That was it. Close The Doors; it's all over.

PAMELA SUSAN COURSON

Pamela Courson—who had long ago taken to calling herself Pamela Morrison—died on April 25, 1974. She died in her apartment in Hollywood of a heroin overdose. She was twenty-seven, the same age Jim Morrison was when he died.

Ray: It's a tragedy that Pam died. But Pamela and Jim are going to go down in the history books as great lovers, and people are going to be writing plays about them. It's Romeo and Juliet, it's Heloise and Abelard. It's Jim and Pam. I loved them both.

When Pamela's family held a memorial service for her, they decided to make it a celebration of both her and Jim, since he never had one in Los Angeles. Ray and Dorothy attended the service, and Ray played a couple of Doors songs on the organ.

Ray: I don't know what I played, but I know I played "When the Music's Over," and Dorothy said, "That was so weird hearing just the organ part." She said it was very strange and very eerie. Perhaps it was, but it was my tribute to the star-crossed lovers.

13 REVIVALS

13 REVIVALS

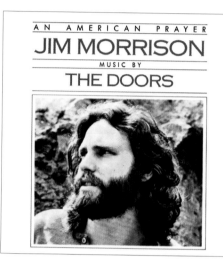

AN AMERICAN PRAYER

Ray: We did this album to show the side of Jim which has been underrated all these years. We wanted the world to be aware that Jim Morrison is a brilliant poet.

It is 1976. The surviving Doors have all moved on, albeit with musical flashbacks to the old days in various bands. Ray Manzarek, after a well-received jazz album, The Golden Scarab (A Rhythm Myth), formed Nite City, a rock band, fronted by Noah James and Paul Warren, which did Doors songs on occasion. Robby Krieger and John Densmore teamed up in The Butts Band; then Robby issued a solo album, Versions, including an instrumental version of "The Crystal Ship." Krieger also has led his own bands, sometimes including his son Waylon on rhythm guitar. Densmore would get into acting, and a one-man show would feature readings from the memoir he would write, Riders on the Storm. In 1995, he was joined onstage at the MET Theater in Hollywood by Manzarek and Krieger, and they jammed on "Roadhouse Blues."

But here in 1976, it is Krieger who, one evening, finds himself thinking about Morrison's poetry, the recordings he made on his birthday at Village Recorders, and how he'd wanted to put music to it. He calls the engineer, John Haeny, to see if he might have a copy of those tapes. He does. In fact, he has the masters.

Robby: John knew that Jim wanted music to be with it. In fact, he'd talked to this classical musician, Fred Miro, and it never happened. So I thought, "Who better to put music to it than us?" That wasn't Jim's idea; he wanted to have something different from The Doors. But after I heard some of the stuff, I knew that we could do something great with it.

Ray: We had about four or five hours of stuff from that session, and we also had some other tapes, outtakes from the live album, so the job was putting it into an album. Jim's words would set off images in your head, and those images would call moods to mind: "Couples naked race down the beach," that sort of thing. I was always seeing things when we played, and this album was the same way, and what we'd try to do is match our music to the pictures that were created in our minds, the collective Doors' mind.

AWAKE
Shake dreams from your hair
My pretty child, my sweet one.
Choose the day and choose the sign of your day
The day's divinity
First thing you see.

(previous spread) The Doors mount
a sonic assault on Los Angeles at the
Hollywood Bowl, 1968

Rolling Stone

SEPTEMBER 17TH, 1981
ISSUE NO. 352
$1.50 UK 80p

Jim Morrison

He's hot,
he's sexy
and he's dead

A vast radiant beach in a cool jeweled moon
Couples naked race down by its quiet side
And we laugh like soft, mad children
Smug in the woolly cotton brains on infancy.
The music and voices are all around us.

After going through the tapes Morrison had left behind, the surviving Doors began work on An American Prayer in 1977.

Ray: Jim came over the earphones when we were laying down the tracks; at a certain point, I'd nod over at John Haeny, and he'd hit the tape that had Jim's voice on it, and in would come Jim on the earphones, just as if he were in the vocal booth, and a couple of times I looked over, as if to go, "Yeah, man, out of sight," and I realized he wasn't there; there was nobody in the vocal booth; it was all in our heads. But his presence was there.

Bill Siddons: When I heard the final record, I was stunned. What they did was what they did from the first time they played together: They took Jim's poetry, which is powerful and unique, but they took it that extra level and made it something that everyone could experience. I believe that the record that they made proves that The Doors, as the three musicians, were Jim's vehicle to reaching people. He would have never accomplished what he did without them...

An American Prayer was released in late 1978. Although the album contained language unsuited for radio airplay (not that it would have received much on mainstream music stations, anyway), it did very well for a spoken-word recording, selling about 250,000 copies and earning The Doors their first nomination for a Grammy.

Doors fans were still out there, Manzarek knew. But, sometimes, it seemed that the band never got the respect it deserved. One day, an announcer on an L.A. radio station was talking about late rock stars of the sixties and mentioned Jimi Hendrix and Janis Joplin as two of the greatest. Ray couldn't believe what he hadn't heard.

Ray: It's like, "Jimi and Janis." Where's *Jim?* Do The Doors even exist? What about "Light My Fire" and all the rest? So that was one of the motivating factors. Danny Sugerman and I said to each other, Jim's not

recognized enough. It's been a couple of years after his death; here's what we're going to do. We are going to make sure that the world knows Jim Morrison. You can like him or dislike him, but you're going to know who he is.

We did interviews. I started to publicize the *Golden Scarab,* and people would invariably ask, "Would you talk about The Doors?" So I just started talking about The Doors, and little by little, you begin to find out that people are fascinated by Jim Morrison.

Danny Sugerman: We decided that with the poetry album out and the book (his and Jerry Hopkins's) coming out, we would develop a radio special and a greatest hits package to cover the recording, print, and radio mediums.

*The book, **No One Here Gets Out Alive**, was the first exhaustive biography of Jim Morrison, told by Hopkins, a journalist who'd become an acquaintance, if not a drinking buddy, and Sugerman, a Doors employee who remained a loyalist to the end. (He became manager of The Doors' musical and business interests until he died of lung cancer in 2005.) Add the uncredited editing of Ran Manzarek himself, and the result was an insider's look at—and, sometimes, psychoanalyses of—one of the most brilliant and tragically flawed stars in rock history.*

The book was preceded, by a year, by the breathtaking use of "The End" in Francis Ford Coppola's Apocalypse Now. As Manzarek had noted about that day on the beach in Venice, Morrison was a pioneer in melding the theme of death into rock 'n' roll. Coppola showed that it was a timeless theme; that it could resonate wherever there were shadows and darkness.

And then there was the Rolling Stone magazine cover of September, 1981: He's hot, he's sexy, and he's dead...

John: Well, I thought, "He's hot, he's sexy, he's dead" was tasteless, but amusing.

Rolling Stone *reported that in 1980, every album in The Doors' catalog doubled or tripled its sales over the previous year. Said Joe Smith*

who was Elektra's chairman (Jac Holzman sold his label to Kinney/ Warner Communications in 1970): "No group that isn't around any more has sold that well for us."

Oh, but The Doors were all around. The Hopkins/Sugerman book spurred interest from Hollywood, and a long string of attempts at turning The Doors' story into a major motion picture began, with producer Allan Carr making the first attempt, and with interested parties over the years, including Brian DePalma, Jerry Weintraub, Irving Azoff, Martin Scorsese, Francis Ford Coppola, Ron Howard, and Oliver Stone. Although Stone was the last director standing, he actually was one of the first to have the idea for a Doors movie. He said he once pitched a screenplay to Morrison himself.

Actors mentioned as possible Jim Morrisons included Richard Gere, Keanu Reeves, Tom ("You had me at 'Hello, I Love You'") Cruise, Jason Patric, and John Travolta. Musicians considered for the role included INXS's Michael Hutchence and U2's Bono, who often did a Doors medley in concert.

Late in 1981, on the tenth anniversary of Jim's death, Robby, Ray, and John went to Père Lachaise.

Robby: It was weird; sad, but it was kind of cool in a way. It was a living grave. People would bring flowers and whisky bottles and all kinds of stuff.

Ray: It was a horrible experience. Yeah, he's fucking dead and he's down there. It's like you go and pay your respects. *Pay my respects!* My respects are "Light My Fire" and "Riders on the Storm" and "Summer's Almost Gone." Those are my respects. I don't want to go there and stand on his grave. He's always with me.

John Densmore first visited the grave in 1975. Back in his hotel room, he found himself writing a letter to Jim—an unsparing, scathing letter wracked with pain and guilt. He had a lot of questions, he said, and he carried his monologues into his book, **Riders on the Storm**. The device, he agreed, was a way to say the things he never told Morrison

John: Originally the letter was my heart, my sadness, visiting him at the grave, and then I realized, as I was writing the book, that I could do this; I could drop this in whenever I feel like talking to Jim, and I could say some things that I've wanted to say to him, and I'm older now, and maybe I didn't have the nerve to say to him.

And I even addressed his demise. I was a little critical. I said, "What you missed was that the sacred needs to be transformed to an inner cathedral." I was saying that he got the spirit out of the bottle, and he had to bring it inside. But we didn't have substance abuse clinics then, and I didn't know he had a disease, so yeah, it felt good to say some things to him. And certainly if some younger kids heard them too, that ain't bad.

Anne: Why is Jim an icon today? One reason is that he never got old. And he was going through that rebel time, that exciting time in your life when you're reaching out and being everything you can be. And maybe people see that in him. "Search for your artistry" or something. I don't know. I'm amazed.

Adm. Morrison: We look back on him with great delight—his career and we knew him as a boy, it was a great pleasure. The fact that he's dead is unfortunate, but looking back on his life, it's a very pleasant thought.

I had no idea of his popularity not only in the U.S. but also in Europe; it taught me that he was almost an international star. That was good to know. I should have known it.

OLIVER STONE'S *THE DOORS*

After a decade of bouncing from one producer to another, from one studio to another, and involving dozens of potential directors, writers, and stars, the Doors movie got made. Oliver Stone, of Platoon *and* Born on the Fourth of July *and* Wall Street, *did it, and the movie, released in spring of 1991, was, no doubt about it, a Stone production, as in brimstone and hellfire.*

As Morrison, a convincing Val Kilmer slashed his way through the movie, wielding either a microphone or a bottle. Pamela, played by

Meg Ryan, was a cartoon girlfriend, albeit a feisty one, whining and screaming at him. The Doors were mostly one-dimensional figures in the background. The concert scenes were convincing, and Stone bought Morrison's childhood memory—or tale—of his encounter with Indians, and sold it to the movie audience, making it—along with a physical being representing death—a running subtheme.

As movies are wont to do, **The Doors** *played fast and fancy with even the most basic facts. Stone gave Ray and Dorothy Manzarek a daughter they don't have. He had Morrison, on* **The Ed Sullivan Show,** *defiantly snarling out the forbidden word "higher, yeah!" when Jim simply sang the word. He had Morrison telling reporters that his father ran "into a truckload of Navajos" on the highway. He clustered several characters into one woman, had her involving Jim in a blood-drinking ritual, and gave her a real name: Patricia Kennealy. The writer was not pleased, and sniped at Stone throughout her book. So did Ray Manzarek, who, along with the rest of The Doors, had been interviewed for the script. (Densmore and Krieger had cameos, while Kennealy was given the role of a priestess conducting the Wicca wedding of Jim and the Patricia character.)*

Ray: The story is so good and so exciting! It's The Doors, these four individual guys realizing the American dream, interwoven with the story of the sixties—the assassinations, the love-ins, the politics, the feminism, the black power, and the Vietnam War—what a great movie that would have made! And the psychological deterioration and ultimate degeneration of Jim Morrison. But at the end, the redemption through *L.A. Woman,* and he's off to Paris! That's what I told Oliver Stone, but he didn't hear that; he wanted to make some sex and drugs and rock 'n' roll, white powder, glass-pipe movie fueled by tequila. That's the problem. Where's the funny Jim Morrison? Where's the charming Jim Morrison? Where's the humor? The Doors never laugh in the movie. As potheads, we laughed a lot.

This isn't the story of The Doors. It's the evil side of sex and drugs. You want to know what I think? Oliver Stone was over there in Vietnam and the hippies were back here smoking dope and making love, not war, and he was jealous. Oliver Stone is using The Doors movie to get even.

John: Robby and I were of the opinion that this is a major Hollywood director, we'd better give him all the info we can, which we did. I love him for giving it a go. When we were at the Avalon Ballroom in San Francisco, he was in a bunker in Vietnam. He's trying to play catch-up, and that's good. Oliver said, "If you don't like my foot on your chest, don't go to my movies." He knows he's rough, and he's great.

I always say, "Well, I don't remember all those naked girls running up onstage. We would have stopped playing! So a third of it's fiction. Amy Madigan, the actress and Ed Harris' wife, is a friend of mine. She said, "John, they're going to take your six-year career, they're going to cram it into two hours, and blow it up the size of a two-story building. Is that going to be reality? You're going to have to let it go."

I was a little disappointed that the movie wasn't more about the sixties, when the seeds of civil rights, the peace movement, and feminism were all planted, and it wasn't just a bunch of hippies smoking dope. And there's a moment on the beach with Jim and Ray, saying, "Things are changing. We've gotta go for it." And he didn't put that in the movie. The movie's about a self-destructive artist, and Oliver's in that area. It's a director's movie, and for that I think it's pretty good.

And I think Val Kilmer should have gotten nominated for an Oscar. I was on the set, and he was *frightening;* gave me chills, I thought Jim was back.

Robby: I thought Val Kilmer did a great job, and I thought, "Hell, it could have been a lot worse. There was stuff wrong with it, but overall I was pretty happy. I thought it was a great rock 'n' roll movie. Possibly the best one I've ever seen.

Ray: That Oliver Stone thing did real damage to the guy I knew: Jim Morrison the poet.

But a lot of people loved the movie. A lot of girls found it romantic—that Val Kilmer thing—romantic and dangerous. And maybe that fits the mood of the times we're in.

Andy Morrison: I was OK with the movie. I was uncomfortable with Val Kilmer, but the second time I saw it he looked better. At first, it just didn't quite look right; Jim was a lot easier going and laughing and liked to tell a joke here and have a good time. It wasn't Val's fault, but Jim was a lot easier going and not quite as mystic.

Whatever he was, people are forming their impressions of Morrison and The Doors based on a movie. They read books and magazine articles that range from knowledgeable to pulp fiction. They go to Père Lachaise and to landmarks in Hollywood. The Whisky still stands, as does, of all things, the Alta Cienega Motel, where the $10 rooms now go for $65, and where they'll tell you which was Jim's room. On Norton Avenue, near Havenhurst, the apartment he shared, sometimes, with Pamela has a sign in front, as if it's one of those eighteenth-century buildings in New Orleans:

**LAST U.S. HOME
JIM MORRISON**

It wasn't before, but, these days, the driveway up to the apartment is gated.

RIDERS ON THE STORM

Soon after Oliver Stone had his say, Ray Manzarek had his. Having directed two Doors videos, Dance on Fire and Live at the Hollywood Bowl, he now put together and directed The Soft Parade, a compilation of news and video clips. Manzarek began by calling the movie "atrocious" and saying he wanted to show "the real Jim Morrison. This is the artist, the poet."

The other Doors did not join in the raking of Stone. And although they did the commentary for The Doors Collection, a DVD compilation of the three videos, there soon would be strains in their relationship. John published his memoirs, Riders on the Storm, in 1991, and Ray did not take kindly to John's characterizations of him and, in particular, of Jim Morrison. In 1999, Manzarek wrote his own story, Light My Fire: My Life with The Doors.

And, in more recent years, the three surviving Doors found themselves in a legal tussle over the band's name.

They had not performed together since their jam at Densmore's reading in Hollywood in 1995. Before that, they were inducted into the Rock and Roll Hall of Fame in Los Angeles in 1993, and played "Roadhouse Blues," "Break On Through," and "Light My Fire," with Pearl Jam's Eddie Vedder handling lead vocals.

In 2000, they played together on a couple of tracks of Stoned Immaculate, a tribute to The Doors produced by Ralph Sall. He gathered a disparate group of artists, from poet William S. Burroughs and blues legend John Lee Hooker to newer alt rockers like Stone Temple Pilots, Creed, and Days of the New. Aerosmith performed "Love Me Two Times," while Perry Farrell of Jane's Addiction and Exene from X, the great punk-rock band that once worked with Manzarek, were backed by all three Doors on an original track called "Children of Night."

In 2001, Manzarek, Krieger, and Densmore had participated in the music channel VH1's Storytellers series. They talked about the band and how some of their songs came to be, and performed those numbers behind a parade of contemporary rock singers. All of them had played on the Stone Immaculate CD: Perry Farrell; Ian Astbury of The Cult, Scott Weiland of Stone Temple Pilots, Pat Monahan of Train, and Scott Stapp of Creed.

Song after song, The Doors demonstrated the timelessness of their music, and singer after singer showed that one could perform the band's classics without impersonating Jim Morrison.

Robby: My manager, Tom Vitorino, was talking with his friends at Harley-Davidson, and they were having their one hundredth anniversary party, and they wanted The Doors. Stuff like that had been offered before, but we just didn't feel like it was time to do it. But we'd done *VH1 Storytellers,* and that proved to us that it could work. So we figured, why not? We know the audience likes it, and whenever I play with my band, people would come up and ask, "Hey, when are you guys going to get back together and play? It's been too long."

Krieger said he and Ray invited John to participate, but that John declined. For one thing, he suffered from the ear ailment, tinnitus; for another, he and Manzarek had traded barbs—and more—in their respective memoirs.

Robby: I wanted John to do it, but he didn't want to do it, and he said, "Oh, you guys go ahead and do it." I thought, "Well, OK. I knew we could do it because we were using my drummer and my bass player, who were already in the Robby Krieger Band. We'd been doing a few Doors

songs already, so all we had to do was plug Ray in there, along with Ian Astbury.

The Harley-Davidson show was a smash, and Ray and Robby accepted bookings for more concerts as The Doors. John took legal action, saying his former bandmates could not use the band's name without his approval. "It shouldn't be called The Doors if there's someone other than Jim singing," he argued. The Morrison and Courson estates also took legal action. Manzarek and Krieger now call their band Riders on the Storm and continue to tour.

Ray: We're honoring Jim Morrison as a poet and artist. Ian Astbury is a great singer who is keeping Jim's words alive. And that's what we do with Riders on the Storm. We keep The Doors' music alive.

In the course of the legal battle, Densmore met Admiral Steve Morrison. In their time together, he got a sense of healing.

John: This was the target of "Father, I want to kill you"…the person we projected all negativity onto because he was literally fighting in the Vietnam War, and his son was gone, and here I was, a peer. Jim said they were dead and I'm sure that hurt them. So he's coming to protect his son's legacy; I'm his son's peer, so there's a perfect ingredient for a healing of the sixties.

He put out his hand and said, "Sorry it's under these circumstances, but it's great to meet you." There was a warmth. He was coming to bat for his son. It was unspoken, but for several days we had a chance to get together for lunch. He didn't say much, but his sister did. She said "Well, did he tease you as much as he did us?"

We were all commiserating over this great, tortured artist, and that felt good, kind of like group therapy.

Densmore knew something about therapy. His brother Jim committed suicide in 1978.

John: I found a group called Survivors of Suicide. No one had to say anything. Just sitting there with people who'd gone through what I did was healing. Being with your peers—you can just feel better. "Someone

(below) The Doors, up in San Francisco for a gig at the Avalon, photographed in the Muir Woods, 1967

For all that John has said, and continues to say, about the difficulties of working with Jim Morrison, he would not have had his career go any other way.

John: I'm so thankful that I hooked onto this avenue of creativity, that my job was something I was so passionate about, and still am.

It was like a fantastic dream. Sometimes I don't know if it was true. "Of The Doors" is permanently etched on my forehead—which is a good thing.

I'm very proud of the band. I was the drummer in a big group, I mean a *big* group. In the sixties there were a lot of groups, and we're still around and they aren't.

Jim was so smart, but that got him. But what a great guy. I'm just very thankful to have been an accompanist to this great artist. Tortured, but great. He gave a lot. He had to.

Densmore is married to documentary filmmaker Leslie Neale; they live in Santa Monica, his hometown, and John continues to play music, with an Afro-jazz ensemble, Tribaljazz. Among its repertoire is "Riders on the Storm," with horns, vibes, John's drums, and a barely whispered reading of its lyrics.

Meantime, the Riders on the Storm play on.

Robby: I've had more fun doing this in the last three years than in the old days because in the old days it was great and everything, but with Jim it was always such a question mark that it was nerve-wracking, and with Ian you know what you're going to get; it's going to be great every night and maybe not quite as exciting here and there, but the bad part about it in those days was the bad shows. That wasn't really fair to the audience. That was their gamble. Were they going to catch us on a good night?

Ray: I don't really flash back, although in Paris—Jim's birthday is December 8, and we were there at his grave on December 8 in 2003, when he would have been sixty. The graveyard was filled with people. We lit some of his poetry on fire, sent the smoke up to the heavens, incense, flowers, with cameras going off. We played that night at a little nightclub, a secret show that obviously wasn't a secret, as people jammed into the place.

The next night, we played one of the bigger auditoriums, and we played all of *L.A. Woman,* the first time we ever did that—it was a birthday present to Jim—and then we got into the last song of the set, "L.A. Woman," and it was so good, I lost myself, I was gone. Ian is singing, and Phil Chen on bass and Ty "The Monster" Dennis on drums are just kicking the thing at an impossible tempo, my eyes are closed, my head is shaking back and forth, I'm hypnotizing myself, and I saw Jim's grave in my mind's eye and a hand came out of the grave like *Carrie,* but it was all positive, and it was Jim's hand, and he said, "Don't stop, Ray, wait for me, keep on going, don't stop, I'm coming!" And it was just like, "What has just gone through my mind?!!!"

That's the power of the music, to take you to other places, and I went shaman, which I don't do. I was laughing and crying at the same time, and Ian is singing, and Robby is soloing over the top of it, and I'm just playing as fast as I can. What a moment!

Together or apart, whether playing classic Doors songs or exploring new sounds, Ray Manzarek, Robby Krieger, and John Densmore cannot escape their legacy, or the memory of that young, handsome acidhead who'd never sung before, and who took them on the trip of their lives.

He is with them still. And not just them. As Manzarek wrote:

Jim is always with us. In the air, in the ether, in the electricity. In the sounds and rhythms of Doors music. In the images of his poetry. In the joys and anguish of his soul, which he so publicly bared to us. In the hundreds of photos of the "young lion" that wink out at us from the collective media. In the radios playing of "Riders on the Storm" on rainy days. In a blurb in a newspaper, or a book title, or a film title using one of his lines, one of his catchphrases. And his face on the T-shirts being sold from Venice Beach, California, to San Marco Square in Venice, Italy. I have seen them. And in each new generation's discovery of The Doors and Jim's plea of: "Please, please, listen to me, children. You are the ones who will rule the world." In each new generation's quest for its own freedom, Jim is there. The Doors are there.

14 THE DOORS' MUSICAL IMPACT: ENDLESS
by Steve Baltin

14 THE DOORS' MUSICAL IMPACT: ENDLESS

by Steve Baltin

The Doors remain an undeniable presence today. You hear it and see it everywhere you turn in today's music. System of a Down's guitarist/architect Daron Malakian says that without The Doors, there may have been no System. "The Doors impacted a big amount of the vision that is behind System of a Down," he says. "System of a Down is a poem that I wrote called 'Victims of a Down,' and I never wrote poetry before I got into The Doors."

"I don't think my music would be the same without the Doors," says Scott Weiland, a key force in both Stone Temple Pilots and Velvet Revolver. "The Doors were a huge influence on me, especially Morrison vocally."

The Doors' music, says Tom Hamilton of Aerosmith, "is part of the well that I drink from."

And Dave Navarro, one-time guitarist for the Red Hot Chili Peppers and Jane's Addiction, says The Doors continue to influence him. "There is a spirit within The Doors that, once it gets in you, you can't lose it, and it affects everything you do."

Even in those who don't recognize the influence of The Doors, Malakian says that it exists. For one thing, The Doors paved the way for the ethos of punk rock. "I've always thought that The Doors opened the door, along with The Rolling Stones, to a certain punk-rock attitude. Whether it's in the lyrics or the stage, him getting arrested onstage … even his death. The shock value that goes into that—that's all what makes punk rock."

"It was that mysterious sound, that eerie, almost frightening sound," says Weiland. "You hear it in Zeppelin, you heard it all the way through Jane's Addiction, and it influenced STP; it influences Velvet Revolver … it's kind of where blues, rock 'n' roll, and art rock collide. And I think they were really the first band to do that."

Today's musicians also note the uniqueness of The Doors' sound. Says Ben Harper: "Not often enough, except in (musical) gear magazines, and tech heads, do people actually acknowledge that there has been no one before or after with that production that sounded anything like that. It was just super unique, which is kind of a mundane statement to make, but no one even tries to imitate it, it's just so blatantly The Doors."

"It's not like they sounded like twenty other bands from that era," says Joe Perry of Aerosmith. "They had new rules for bass and keyboards and their roots were in jazz, but they played some blues. If you look at Chuck Berry's band, it was the same thing."

Whitestarr lead singer Cisco Adler adds: "There's a real rawness to The Doors that I think you just identify with. It's kind of like the ultimate soundtrack score, the way it rumbles and keeps you going."

Rob Thomas, lead singer for Matchbox 20 and solo artist, believes that's because The Doors have influenced so many different styles of music. "The beginnings of alternative and goth are deep into The Doors. But so was hippie jam band stuff, pop music, and a little metal. Maybe nobody ever seemed to get The Doors down because they were so many different things that people were just taking pieces of them."

(left) Ray and Jim deep into the music at Ondine, New York City, 1966

As it has been since the first Doors revival in the early eighties, the band's catalog remains an enormous seller worldwide. It doesn't hurt that songs such as "Light My Fire," "Touch Me," "Hello, I Love You," "The End," "L.A. Woman," and "Riders on the Storm" are still staples on classic rock radio.

"There are not really any dogs in their catalog," says Frank Black, who, as leader of the Pixies, helped father modern alternative rock. "It's all really great stuff. It's all vital, it's all entertaining, it's all exciting. I never get bored listening to The Doors."

"They have great pop hits and they have great, seemingly never-ending jams," says Dave Navarro. "Get into *American Prayer,* and you can use your mind listening to something like that. You can listen to a couple of tracks off the first record and be on AM radio," Navarro says. "There's a song for every person, a mood for everybody."

Tom Morello, formerly of Rage Against the Machine and current guitarist for Audioslave, believes that diversity is part of what makes The Doors so special.

"There was a depth and an artistic ambition to The Doors that was unique. Jim Morrison very much saw himself as a poet as opposed to a song lyricist and the band as a means of channeling visions from the dark recesses of his mind. And that's very different from bands that are trying to write a hit. But what The Doors had, in addition to that, was the ability to write hits. Hooky. And that was around the time that I began to play guitar too. And there was the [riff]," Morello says, humming the opening of "Love Me Two Times." "We were all trying to learn that riff!"

Though the music is sometimes eclipsed by the myth that surrounds the band and their iconic lead singer, Frank Black believes that The Doors stand up to fellow legends like Led Zeppelin and The Rolling Stones.

"The Doors are one of the few bands that have taken their cue from American blues and then done something with it and taken it to their own place, while still being very heavily committed to it," Black says. "Everything about them was captivating."

Joe Perry names The Doors as one of very few American bands he really liked. "Most bands were like that West Coast hippie stuff, and I just didn't have much use for that kind of music. I really liked the heavy, distorted electric things coming out of England, and it was easy to have The Doors' records right next to the Yardbirds."

Even at a young age, Jane's Addiction front man Perry Farrell knew that The Doors were special. "Eight years old … I already knew what was going on. There's something inherent about The Doors and what they stood for and what they sounded like that I knew that this was the good stuff, that this was worth keeping. So I kept The Doors around me my whole life," he says. "My first car had an eight-track and so I got my hands on a couple of eight-tracks that I would use to basically drive all over—to high school, go out on my dates with and stuff—and one of those eight-tracks was *The Doors' Greatest Hits.* It's like a piece of clothing that you keep practically your whole life; there are probably jackets in your closet that you'll never get rid of, right? That's The Doors."

Alex Orbison, son of rock legend Roy Orbison and drummer for Whitestarr, says The Doors are one of those bands he grew up with. "It was just always played around the house."

Chester Bennington, lead singer of Linkin Park, was in seventh grade in Arizona when he heard The Doors on the radio. In the foreword he wrote for this book, he tells about singing with a buddy in his garage. "For a while," he says, "I thought I was Jim Morrison."

Cynics might say Morrison is a testament to dying young and staying pretty. Others believe the honesty and passion with which Morrison sang and lived made him a rock god before death made him an immortal.

Snoop Dogg remixed "Riders on the Storm" in 2005. The Doors' sincerity is what appeals to him. "When it was expressed it was a true feeling and, once from the heart, it don't have no time limit," Snoop says.

Ray Manzarek, Michael McClure, and many others considered Jim Morrison a poet. Funk king George Clinton and rock star Axl Rose agree. "They were basically a jazz group with a poet," says Clinton.

Rose says he admired Morrison's lyrical prowess. "It was the poetry that did it for me."

"It seems like he was baring his soul," says Aaron Lewis, lead singer of Staind. "The way he sang, the meaning and the feeling and the passion that he put into portraying those words."

Perry Farrell believes that the conviction behind The Doors made them the greatest show on earth. "They were just such a remarkable group that they weren't going to be denied. And they had the power back then, because people really, truly did believe in the power of music. That was an era where these people were not simply celebrities; these people were leaders. These people spoke for their generation, poetically, and that was what their importance was."

They were, in short, revolutionaries, says Tom Morello. "There was definitely a revolutionary component to it, and the idea of overthrowing previous ways of doing things. And that's when culture can give revolution a push in that way, without having to sing songs about the union. I think The Doors were very much a part of questioning everything."

"Music was such a political statement and The Doors were right on the front of that," Joe Perry remembers. "It was really about us against them in those days, about the music, about the uptightness of America and other parts of the world where the establishment was losing its grip. The old ideas weren't working anymore. Music was a symbol and very often rock concerts were the gathering place for those kind of ideas. It was about gathering together people who thought the same, and that was the big difference. The Doors were at the front of that."

Though The Doors came to symbolize the sixties, they transcend that era. The music is finding a new life today in the remix world, by way of several leading dance artists. The members of The Crystal Method, who remixed "Roadhouse Blues," say the two sounds melded seamlessly. "The combination of the two worlds coming together worked really, really well," says the duo's Scott Kirkland.

Paul Oakenfold, who took a turn at "L.A. Woman," says Morrison's vocals are a natural fit for dance beats. "There are very few rock 'n' roll singers, from my experience of mixing a lot of rock records, from The Stones to U2, who have soul. And Morrison has soul; he can sing on an electronic rhythm, and you can bring that soul out."

Given how successfully The Doors fit in with contemporary music, it's no surprise that today's artists believe The Doors would be a success if they were a new band on the scene.

"If it came out today, it would be fucking amazing," says Chester Bennington. "It would be just as amazing as it was when it came out then. They're one of the biggest bands in the world. Certain types of music and certain groups will go on forever."

"Morrison was a rock star unparalleled," says Scott Weiland. "The kind of person that every magazine would be clamoring to speak to. So yeah, they would be huge. I would say on the level of U2 or something. If they came out right now, I think it would probably save rock 'n' roll."

STEVE BALTIN is an entertainment journalist who, during the last decade, has covered music and other forms of pop culture for the *Los Angeles Times, Rolling Stone, Mojo*, the *Chicago Tribune*, and dozens of other publications. In addition to his work on *The Doors By The Doors*, he's contributed to the Music Hound Rock Guide and wrote Linkin Park's bestselling book *From the Inside: Linkin Park's Meteora*.

(below left) Robby in the studio recording Strange Days Los Angeles, 1967

(below right) Ray: "Jim and I having fun in New York," 1967

(following page left) John digs into a press-roll in NY, 1967

(following page right) Jim in the studio in Los Angeles, 1967

(below) Under the Golden Gate Bridge,
San Francisco, 1967

(below) In full throttle, at Steve Paul's The
Scene, New York City, 1967

(below and right) Jim Morrison in the subway, New York City, 1968

(below) Jim as Nijinski the Dancer, 1968

(below) Jim in his railroad pants, onstage
at the Whisky a Go Go, Los Angeles, 1966

(below) Jim smoking a stogie onstage in
New York, 1969

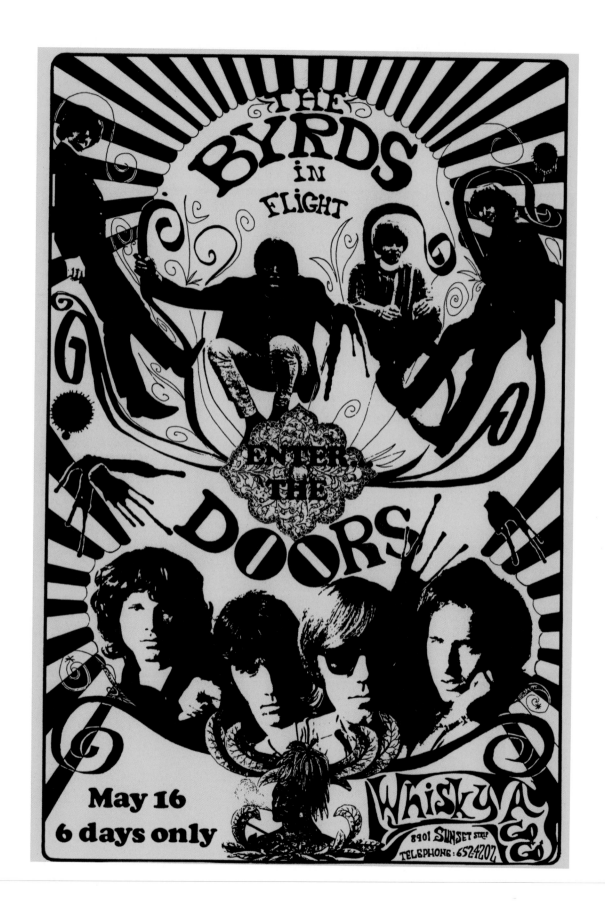

(below) Jim paying homage to Brian
Jones, 1968

(below) Shaman dancing at the
Roundhouse. London, 1968

(below) Ray getting ready to do overdubs
during *The Soft Parade* recording
sessions, 1969

(below) Street denizens out in front of the
original Hard Rock Café at 5th and Main,
Los Angeles, 1970

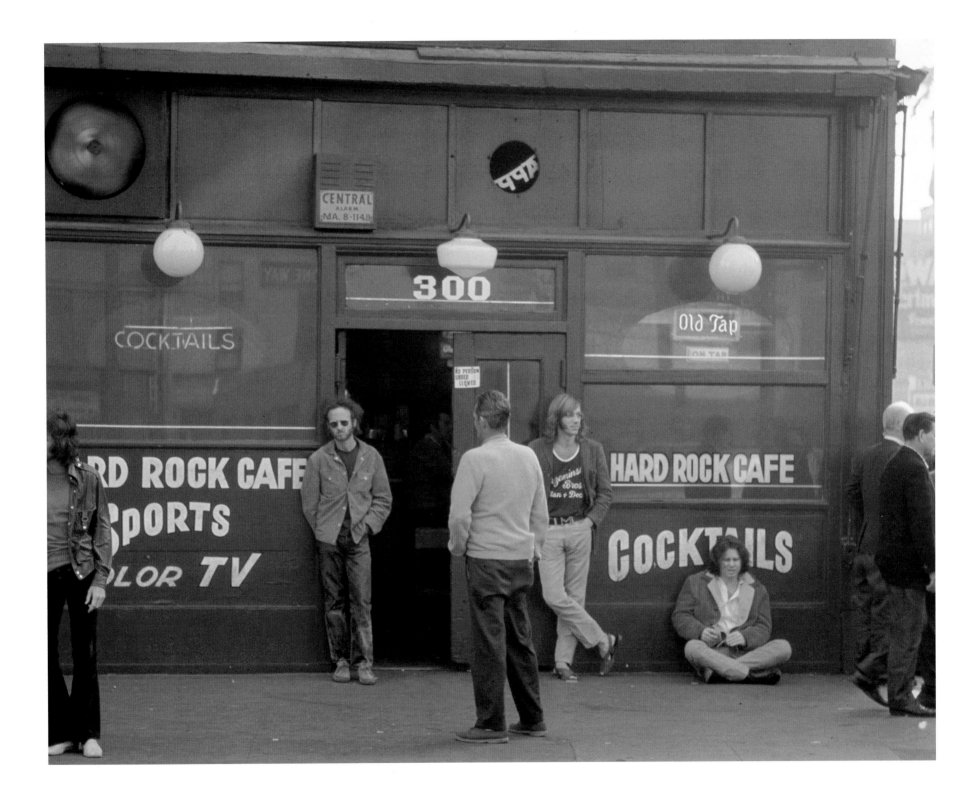

(below and right) Jim at the pyramids,
Teotihuacán Mexico, 1969

(below and right) The Shaman flies, the Shaman crashes. Roundhouse, London, 1968

(below) The Shaman reborn.
Roundhouse, London, 1968

(below) Jim and Pam at the Bronson
Caves, Los Angeles 1970

(below) Ray outside of the Hard Rock
Café, downtown Los Angeles, 1970

(below) Robby outside of the Hard Rock
Café, downtown Los Angeles, 1970

(below and right) Jim, Ray, Robby, and John—The Doors.

DISCOGRAPHY

The Doors—Released on Vinyl January 1967—Elektra/Asylum Records

Strange Days—Released on Vinyl October 1967—Elektra/Asylum Records

Waiting for the Sun—Released on Vinyl July 1968—Elektra/Asylum Records

Soft Parade—Released on Vinyl July 1969—Elektra/Asylum Records

Morrison Hotel—Released on Vinyl February 1970—Elektra/Asylum Records

Absolutely Live—Released on Vinyl July 1970—Elektra/Asylum Records

L.A. Woman—Released on Vinyl April 1971—Elektra/Asylum Records

Other Voices—Released on Vinyl October 1971—Elektra/Asylum Records

Weird Scenes Inside The Goldmine—January 1972—Elektra/Asylum Records

Full Circle—Released on Vinyl July 1972—Elektra/Asylum Records

The Best of the Doors—Quadraphonic Release August 1973—Elektra/Asylum Records

An American Prayer—Released on Vinyl November 1978—Elektra/Asylum Records

Greatest Hits—Initial Release 1980—Elektra/Asylum Records

Alive She Cried—1983—Elektra/Asylum Records

The Best of the Doors—Released on Cassette 1985—Elektra/Asylum Records

Classics—Release on Vinyl 1985—Elektra/Asylum Records

In Concert—Released on CD May 1991—Elektra/Asylum Records

The Doors—Released on Gold CD 1992—DCC Gold

Strange Days—Released on Gold CD 1992—DCC Gold

Waiting for the Sun—Released on Gold CD 1992—DCC Gold

L.A. Woman—Released on Gold CD 1992—DCC Gold

American Prayer—Re-released on CD 1995—Rhino

Absolutely Live—Re-released on CD 1996—Rhino

Greatest Hits—Released on CD October 1996—Rhino

The Doors Box Set—Released on CD October 1997—Rhino

Complete Studio Recordings (Box)—1999—Rhino

Bright Midnight Sampler—Released on CD September 25 2000—Bright Midnight Archives/Rhino

Live in Detroit—Released on CD October 23 2000—Bright Midnight Archives/Rhino

L.A. Woman—Released on DVDA 2000—Elektra/Asylum Records

No One Here Gets Out Alive—Released on CD—November 20 2000—Bright Midnight Archives/Rhino

The Lost Interview Vol. 1—Released on CD—April 16 2001—Bright Midnight Archives/Rhino

Live at the Aquarius Theatre: The First Performance—Released On CD May 7 2001—Bright Midnight Archives/Rhino

Live in Hollywood: HIghlights from the Aquarius Theatre Performances—Released on CD May 7 2001—Bright Midnight Archives/Rhino

Live at the Aquarius (2nd performance)—Released on CD September 24 2001—Bright Midnight Archives/Rhino

The Lost Interview Vol. 2—Released on CD—November 12 2001—Bright Midnight Archives/Rhino

Backstage And Dangerous—Released on CD—November 12 2001—Bright Midnight Archives/Rhino

Legacy: The Absolute Best—Released on CD—August 12 2003—Rhino

Boot Yer Butt—Released on CD—November 25 2003—Bright Midnight Archives/Rhino

Live in Philadelphia—Released on CD November 29 2005—Bright Midnight Archives/Rhino

Love, Death, Travel—Released on CD January 2006—Rhino Handmade

SELECTED BIBLIOGRAPHY

BOOKS, MAGAZINES, AND NEWSPAPERS

Babitz, Eve. "Jim Morrison Is Dead and Living in Hollywood." *Esquire,* March, 1991.

Balfour, Victoria. *Rock Wives.* New York: William Morrow & Co./Beech Tree Books, 1986.

Breslin, Rosemary. "Jim Morrison, 1981: Renew My Subscription to the Resurrection." *Rolling Stone,* September 17, 1981.

Burks, John. "Uh-Oh, I Think I Exposed Myself Out There." *Rolling Stone,* April 5, 1969.

Butler, Patricia. *The Tragic Romance of Pamela and Jim Morrison.* London: Omnibus Press, 1998.

Chorush, Bob. "Jim Morrison on Trial." *L.A. Free Press,* September 4, 1970.

Crisafulli, Chuck. *When the Music's Over.* New York: Thunder Mouth Press, 2000.

Cuscuna, Michael. "Behind the Doors." *Downbeat,* May 28, 1970.

Davis, Stephen. *Jim Morrison: Life, Death, Legend.* New York: Gotham Books, 2004.

Densmore, John. *Riders on the Storm.* New York: Dell Publishing, 1990.

Des Barres, Pamela. *I'm with the Band.* New York: William Morrow & Co./Beech Tree Books, 1987.

Didion, Joan. "Waiting for Morrison." *Saturday Evening Post,* March 9, 1968.

Doe, Andrew and Tobler, John. *In Their Own Words: The Doors.* London: Omnibus Press, 1988.

Diehl, Digby. "Love & the Demonic Psyche." *Eye,* April, 1968.

Fein, Art. *The L.A. Musical History Tour.* Winchester, Massachusetts: Faber and Faber, 1990.

Fong-Torres, Ben. "Jim Morrison's Got the Blues." *Rolling Stone,* March 4, 1971.

Fong-Torres, Ben. "James Douglas Morrison, Poet: Dead at 27." *Rolling Stone,* August 5, 1971.

Fong-Torres, Ben. "Paris." *BAM,* July 3, 1981.

Gilmore, Mikal. "The Unforgettable Fire." *Rolling Stone,* August 30, 2001.

Gilmore, Mikal. "The Legacy of Jim Morrison and The Doors." *Rolling Stone,* April 4, 1991.

Harris, Jeane. "Writers on the Storm: An Evening with John Densmore and Friends." *Doors Collectors Magazine,* spring/summer 1996.

Hochman, Steve. "A Taste of Vintage Whisky." *Los Angeles Times,* January 18, 1999.

Holzman, Jac and Daws, Gavan. *Follow The Music.* Santa Monica, Calif.: FirstMedia Books, 1998.

Hopkins, Jerry. *Hit & Run: The Jimi Hendrix Story,* Perigree Books, 1983

Hopkins, Jerry and Sugerman, Danny. *No One Here Gets Out Alive.* New York: Warner Books Inc., 1980.

Hopkins, Jerry. *The Lizard King.* New York: Macmillan Publishing Company, 1991.

Hopkins, Jerry. "The Doors on Stage: Assaulting the Libido." *Rolling Stone,* February 10, 1968.

Hopkins, Jerry. "Jim Morrison Is Alive and Well All Over the Place." *Rolling Stone,* September 17, 1981.

Jackson, Blair. "Paul Rothchild." *BAM,* July 3, 1981.

James, Lizze. "Jim Morrison: Ten Years Gone." *Creem,* 1981.

Jones, Dylan. *Jim Morrison: Dark Star.* New York: Viking Studio Books, 1991.

Kennealy, Patricia. *Strange Days.* New York: Plume/Penguin, 1993.

Kogut, Galen. "Busted in Miami: Was It Political or Even Legal?" *Doors Collectors Magazine,* Fall 1993.

Lisciandro, Frank. *A Feast of Friends.* New York: Warner Books Inc., 1991.

Lisciandro, Frank. *An Hour For Magic.* New York: Delilah Books, 1982.

Mahoney, Larry. "Rock Group Fails to Stir a Riot." *Miami Herald,* March 3, 1969.

Manzarek, Ray. *Light My Fire.* New York: Berkley Boulevard, 1999.

Modderman, Rainer. "Jim Morrison's Quiet Days in Paris," based in part on *The Doors.* Koningswinter, Germany: Heel Verlag, 1990.

Morrison, Jim. *The Lords and the New Creatures.* New York: Simon and Schuster, 1969.

Morrison, Jim. *Wilderness: The Lost Writings of Jim Morrison, Volume 1.* New York: Villard Books, 1988.

Morrison, Jim. *The American Night: The Writings of Jim Morrison, Volume 2.* New York: Vintage Books, 1991

Perry, Sara. "John vs. Ray & Robby: The Battle for a Name." *Doors Collectors Magazine,* www.doors.com.

Riordan, James and Prochnicky, Jerry. *Break On Through.* New York: William Morrow & Co.,1991.

Rocco, John (ed.). *The Doors Companion.* New York: Schirmer, 1997.

Saadi, Ed, "The Doors at the Rock and Roll Hall of Fame." *Doors Collectors Magazine,* spring/summer 1997.

Seymore, Bob. *The End: The Death of Jim Morrison.* London: Omnibus Press, 1990.

Shaw, Greg. *The Doors On the Road.* London: Omnibus Press, 1997.

Sims, Judith. "Pam Morrison: A Final Curtain on Her Affair with Life." *Rolling Stone,* June 6, 1974.

Slick, Grace and Cagan, Andrea. *Somebody to Love?* New York: Warner Books, Inc., 1998.

Stephanos, Tarn C. "Blood in the Streets: A New Haven Retrospective." *Doors Collectors Magazine,* spring 1994.

Stevenson, Salli. "An Interview with Jim Morrison." *Circus,* January, 1971 and February, 1971.

Sugerman, Danny. *The Doors: The Illustrated History.* New York: William Morrow and Company, Inc., 1983.

Sugerman, Danny. *The Doors: The Complete Illustrated Lyrics.* New York: Hyperion, 1991.

Vanjak, Gloria. "State of Florida vs. Jim Morrison." *Rolling Stone,* October 1, 1970.

Whitburn, Joel. *Billboard Hot 100 Charts: The Sixties.* Menonomee Falls, Wisc.: Record Research Inc.,1990.

Whitburn, Joel. *The Billboard Book of Top 40 Hits.* New York: Billboard Books, 2000.

Wolfe, Bernard. "The Real-Life Death of Jim Morrison." *Esquire,* June, 1972.

Yanez, Luisa. "Flashback to Jim Morrison's Infamous Miami Concert." *Miami Herald,* March 1, 2006.

AUDIO AND VIDEO

Burden, Gary and Diltz, Henry. *Under the Covers.* Triptych Pictures, Los Angeles, California, 2001.

The Best of The Doors, Universal Home Video, Inc., Los Angeles, California, 1997.

The Doors. *Boot Yer Butt!: The Doors Bootlegs,* Bright Midnight/Rhino Handmade, Los Angeles, California, 2003

The Doors. *The Ceremony Continues,* Tabak Marketing Ltd., London, England, 1992.

The Doors. *The Doors Box Set,* Elektra Entertainment Group, New York, New York, 1997.

The Doors. *The Doors Collection: Dance On Fire/ Live at the Hollywood Bowl / The Soft Parade.* Universal Studios, Los Angeles, California, 1999.

The Doors. *Feast of Friends.* 1969.

The Doors. Live in Philadelphia '70, Bright Midnight/Rhino Handmade, Los Angeles, California, 2005.

The Doors. The Lost Interview Tapes Featuring Jim Morrison, Volume One. Bright Midnight/Rhino Handmade, 2001.

The Doors. *No One Here Gets Out Alive: The Doors' Tribute to Jim Morrison,* Eagle Vision/Eagle Rock Entertainment, 1981.

The Doors of the 21st Century. *L.A. Woman Live,* Image Entertainment, Chatsworth, California, 2003.

The Doors. *Live in Europe:* 1968, Eagle Rock Entertainment Ltd., 2004.

Fong-Torres, Ben. A Conversation With Jim Morrison, Beserkley Records, Berkeley, California, 1997.

Holzman, Jac. *The Doors From the Inside.*

Ladd, Jim. *No One Here Gets Out Alive, Parts I-IV: An Audio Documentary.* Bright Midnight/Rhino Handmade, Los Angeles, California, 2001.

Stone, Oliver. *The Doors.* Canal/Artisan Entertainment, Inc. Santa Monica, California. 1991.

Stoned But Articulate II: Jim Morrison of The Doors, Ozit-Morpheus Records, Nortwich Cheshire, U.K.

Stoned Immaculate: The Music of The Doors, Elektra Entertainment Group, Inc., New York, NY, 2000.

VH1 Storytellers. TheDoors: A Celebration. Viacom International/Image Entertainment, Inc. Chatsworth, California, 2001.

PHOTOGRAPHY CREDITS

page ii Gloria Stavers © DMC
page v © Oddette Sugerman
pages viii–ix Paul Ferrara © DMC
page x Paul Ferrara © DMC (top left)
page x Paul Ferrara © DMC (top right)
page x Paul Ferrara © DMC (top left)
page xi Paul Ferrara © DMC (top right)
page xii Paul Ferrara © DMC (top left)
page xii Paul Ferrara © DMC (top right)
page xiii Paul Ferrara © DMC (top left)
page xiii Paul Ferrara © DMC (top right)
page xiv Wendell Hamick
page xv Paul Ferrara © DMC
page xvii © Henry Diltz
page 1 © Joel Brodsky
page 3 © Joel Brodsky
page 4 Provided by Ray Manzarek
page 6 Provided by Ray Manzarek
page 7 Provided by Ray Manzarek
page 8 Provided by Anne Morrison
page 9 Provided by Anne Morrison
page 11 Provided by Anne Morrison
page 13 Provided by Anne Morrison
page 15 Provided by Ray Manzarek
page 17 © Joel Brodsky
page 18 Provided by John Densmore (top left)
page 18 Provided by John Densmore (bottom left)
page 18 Provided by John Densmore (right)
page 21 © Bobby Klein / Fahey Klein Gallery
page 23 Provided By Robby Krieger
page 24 © Joel Brodsky
page 25 Paul Ferrara © DMC
page 26 Provided by Steve Young
page 26 Provided by Steve Young
page 27 Provided by Steve Young
pages 28–29 © Bobby Klein / Fahey Klein Gallery
page 31 Bill Harvey
page 32 © Bobby Klein / Fahey Klein Gallery
page 34 © Bobby Klein / Fahey Klein Gallery
page 35 © Bobby Klein / Fahey Klein Gallery
page 36 © Bobby Klein / Fahey Klein Gallery
page 39 Bill Harvey
page 40 Bill Harvey
page 41 © Bobby Klein / Fahey Klein Gallery
page 42 © Bobby Klein / Fahey Klein Gallery
page 43 © Bobby Klein / Fahey Klein Gallery

pages 44–45 © Bobby Klein / Fahey Klein Gallery
page 46 © Bobby Klein / Fahey Klein Gallery
page 47 © Bobby Klein / Fahey Klein Gallery
pages 48–49 Paul Ferrara © DMC
page 51 © Bobby Klein / Fahey Klein Gallery
page 52 Don Paulsen © Michael Ochs Archive
page 54 © Bobby Klein / Fahey Klein Gallery
page 55 Paul Ferrara © DMC
page 56 © George Rodriguez
page 57 © George Rodriguez
page 59 Thomas Monaster
page 60 Paul Ferrara © DMC
page 61 © George Rodriguez
page 62 Paul Ferrara © DMC
page 63 © George Rodriguez
page 64 Paul Ferrara © DMC (left)
page 64 © George Rodriguez (right)
page 65 © George Rodriguez
pages 66–67 © James Fortune
page 69 Paul Ferrara © DMC
page 70 © James Fortune
page 72 Paul Ferrara © DMC
page 73 Paul Ferrara © DMC
page 74 Paul Ferrara © DMC
page 76 © Bobby Klein / Fahey Klein Gallery
page 77 Paul Ferrara © DMC (top)
page 77 Provided by Robby Krieger (bottom)
page 78 Don Paulsen © Michael Ochs Archive
page 79 Don Paulsen © Michael Ochs Archive
page 80 Gloria Stavers © DMC
page 81 Jerry Hopkins © DMC
page 82 Tom Copi © Michael Ochs Archive
page 83 © Art Kane Archive
page 84 Gloria Stavers © DMC (left top)
page 84 Gloria Stavers © DMC (left middle)
page 84 Gloria Stavers © DMC (left bottom)
page 84 Photographer Unknown
page 85 © James Fortune
pages 86–87 © Bobby Klein / Fahey Klein Gallery
page 89 Ethan Russell © DMC
page 90 Paul Ferrara © DMC
page 92 Michael Montfort © DMC
page 94 Ethan Russell © DMC
page 95 Ethan Russell © DMC

page 97 Michael Montfort © DMC
page 98 Paul Ferrara © DMC
page 99 © Cal Deal
page 100 © Chuck Boyd / Starfile (left top)
page 100 Ethan Russell © DMC (left middle)
page 100 Joseph Sia © Bill Grahm Archive (left bottom)
page 100 Michael Montfort © DMC (middle)
page 100 Paul Ferrara © DMC (right)
page 101 © Joel Brodsky
pages 102–103 Paul Ferrara © DMC
page 105 Ethan Russell © DMC
page 106 © Ed Caraeff
page 108 Peter Hulbert © DMC
page 110 Peter Hulbert © DMC
page 111 Paul Ferrara © DMC
page 113 Peter Hulbert © DMC
page 114 © Henry Diltz
page 115 Paul Ferrara © DMC
page 116 © Henry Diltz
page 117 © Ed Caraeff
page 119 © Raeanne Rubenstein
page 120 © Raeanne Rubenstein (left)
page 120 © Raeanne Rubenstein (right)
page 121 © Raeanne Rubenstein
page 122 © Henry Diltz (top left)
page 122 © Henry Diltz (bottom left)
page 122 Ethan Russell © DMC (right)
page 123 Paul Ferrara © DMC (left)
page 123 Paul Ferrara © DMC (top right)
page 123 Paul Ferrara © DMC (middle right)
page 123 Paul Ferrara © DMC (bottom right)
pages 124–125 Michael Montfort © DMC
page 127 Anonymous
page 128 Michael Montfort © DMC
page 130 Paul Ferrara © DMC
page 131 © Ed Caraeff
page 132 Michael Montfort © DMC
page 133 Ethan Russell © DMC
page 134 Ethan Russell © DMC
page 135 Ethan Russell © DMC
page 136 Paul Ferrara © DMC
page 137 Ethan Russell © DMC
page 138 Ethan Russell © DMC
page 139 Ethan Russell © DMC
page 140 © Ed Caraeff
page 141 © Ed Caraeff
page 142 © Henry Diltz
page 143 Michael Montfort © DMC

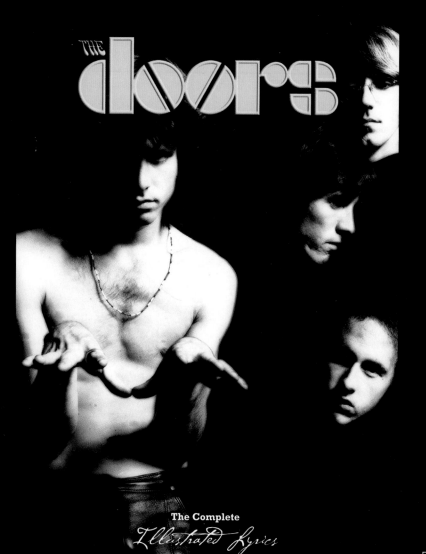

THE DOORS

Perception
BOX SET

Celebrating
THE DOORS 40TH ANNIVERSARY 1967 - 2007

All 6 Studio Albums Expanded to CD+DVD Double Discs.
Every Album Remixed in Stereo & 5.1 Surround Sound.

Features
- 24 RARE & PREVIOUSLY UNRELEASED BONUS TRACKS
- 12 LIVE VIDEO CLIPS
- PHOTO GALLERY
- DISCOGRAPHY
- BRAND-NEW LINER NOTES FOR EACH ALBUM
  WRITTEN BY BEN FONG-TORRES, DAVID FRICKE,
  PAUL WILLIAMS, BARNEY HOSKYNS & BRUCE BOTNICK

IN STORES 11.21.06

Text Doors to 74466*
for official Doors Ringtones including
"BREAK ON THROUGH (TO THE OTHER SIDE)"
"RIDERS ON THE STORM"
"HELLO, I LOVE YOU" *and much more*

www.thedoors.com • www.rhino.com

Elektra

RHINO